QUO'

mall

fore

QUOTE UNQUOTE

German

Edited by
ANTHONY LEJEUNE

STACEY
INTERNATIONAL

089760

Stacey International
128 Kensington Church Street
London W8 4BH
Telephone: +44 (0)20 7221 7166 Fax: +44 (0)20 7792 9288
Email: info@stacey-international.co.uk
www.stacey-international.co.uk

First published by Stacey International in 1998
as part of *The Concise Dictionary of Foreign Quotations*

© Stacey International 2008

ISBN: 978-1-9052-9956-0

Series editor: Anthony Lejeune
Assistant editor: Kitty Carruthers

British Library Cataloguing-in-Publication Data
A catalogue record for this publication is available from
the British Library

PUBLISHER'S PREFACE

Something of the night clings to this nonetheless illuminating little book. If the quotations collected here are united by anything other than their tongue, it is surely the dark Romantic beat of their native heartland. Here the saws and observations of Schiller, Goethe *et al* are brought together under what has become Wagner's 'Wunderreich der Nacht'.

It was, perhaps, the Viennese composer Franz Schubert who, in the course of his prolific *lieder* writing, did more than anyone to amass the shards and fragments of poetry and prose that were soon to join the Western cannon of great snippets.

These Romantic poets, in particular, drew upon the sombre imagery and melancholic vein of nineteenth-century Germanic *angst* (arising in tandem with – and in some measure as a consequence of – the encroachment of industry upon a bucolic landscape of watermills and deep, dark forests). Thus these quotations reveal as much about a national psyche as they do individuals' struggle.

And so we hear Goethe's despairing, 'Ach ich bin des Treibens müde!' ('O, I am tired of the struggle!') – itself perhaps best known today as the opening line to Schubert's *Wandrers Nachtlied*. And we find once more the pain in love, as in Schiller's 'Der Wahn ist kurz, die Rue ist lang' ('The illusion [of love] is brief, the repentance long').

Many of the quotations in these pages are drawn upon worldwide for their ability to sketch, sharply, troubled states of mind. To Goethe, again, and: 'Alles in der Welt läßt sich ertragen, nur nicht eine Reihe von schönen Tagen' ('Everything in the world is bearable, except a series of lovely days').

All this can be seen as surprising in a nation renowned for efficient industriousness. Indeed, amid the yearning, the melancholy and the doubts, we also find no-nonsense realism: 'Der Mensch ist, was er ißt' ('Man is what he eats'); shafts of a collective work-ethic: 'Proletarier aller Länder, vereinigt euch!' (the rallying 'Workers of the world, unite!'); and from a certain twentieth-century invader, that ruthlessly casual enquiry, 'Brennt Paris?' ('Is Paris burning?') – 'something' again, surely, 'of the night'.

Christopher Ind
September 2007

Konrad Adenauer (1876-1967)
Ein Abgrund von Landesverrat.
A bottomless pit of treason.
November 1962, to the Bundestag

Peter Altenberg (1859-1919)
Wie in verwehte Jugendtage blickst du zurück,
Und irgendeiner sagt dir weise: 'Es ist dein Glück!'
Da denkt man, daß es vielleicht so ist,
Wundert sich still, daß man doch nicht froh ist!
As one looks back on the long-gone days of youth,
and somebody wisely tells you: 'You are fortunate!',
you think that perhaps it is true, and are quietly
surprised that you are still not happy!
Sehnsucht

Wenn es in den alten Apfelbäumen rauscht, ist es anders.
Und wenn es in Tannenwipfeln rauscht,ist es anders.
Wenn es über Felder braust, ist es anders.
Wenn es im Weidenbusche rauscht, ist es anders
[Of the wind.]
It's different when it rustles through the old apple
trees; and it's different when it rustles across the tops
of the pine trees. It's different when it roars across the
fields; and it's different when it rustles through the
willow bushes.
Geräsche

Anon

Auf der Welt ist kein Bestand,
Wir müssen alle sterben,
Das ist uns wohlbekannt!
There is no permanence in the world; we must all die
– we are well aware of that!

   Folk song

Ein Kuß von rosiger Lippe,
Und ich fürchte nicht Sturm nicht Klippe!
A kiss from rosy lips, and I fear neither storm nor cliff!

   Folk song

Ein Reich, ein Volk, ein Führer.
One realm, one people, one leader.

   Nazi Party slogan

Ich dien.
I serve.

   Motto of the Prince of Wales, assumed after Crecy by the
   Black Prince, from the banner of the king of Bohemia, who
   had been killed

Ich will in mein Küchel gehn,
Will mein Süpplein kochen,
Steht ein bucklicht Mänlein da,
Hat mein Töpflein brochen.
I want to go into my little kitchen to make my little
soup; a little bent man is standing there who has broken
my little saucepan.

   Folk tale

Kein Feuer, keine Kohle
Kann brennen so heiß
Als heimliche Liebe,
Von der niemand nichts weiß.
No fire nor coals could burn as hotly as the secret love
which no one knows.
    Folk song

Keine Experimente.
No experiments.
    Slogan of the Christian Democrat Party under Adenauer in
    the 1957 election (which they won)

Kinder, Kirche, Küche.
Children, church, kitchen.
    Traditional – the proper concerns for a German woman

Kulturkampf.
Culture struggle.
    Historical name for the struggle with the Clerical Party

Ohne mich.
Without me.
    Slogan of disillusioned post-war German voters

Prosit!
Good luck.
    German toast

Schön ist die Jugend, sie kommt nicht mehr.
Youth is beautiful and will not return.
    Folk song

Sterben, ach! sterben
Soll ich allein!
Oh, I must die alone!
  Folk song

Swes brot ich ezz', des liet ich sing'.
I will sing the song of him whose bread I eat.
  Minstrels' motto

Vorsprung durch Technik.
Progress through technology.
  Advertisement for Audi motors

Wanderjahre.
The years of wandering.
  German expression for the travels of a journeyman after his
  Lehrjahre, the year of apprenticeship

Ernst Arndt (1769-1860)
Zwar der Tapfere nennt sich Herr der Länder
Durch sein Eisen, durch sein Blut.
The brave man calls himself lord of the land through
his iron, through his blood.
  Reputedly the source of Bismarck's phrase

Johannes R. Becher (1891-1958)
Auferstanden aus Ruinen.
Risen from the ruins.
  National anthem of the DDR

Ludwig van Beethoven (1770-1827)

Muß es sein? Es muß sein.

Must it be? It must be.

Georg Berneck

Noch ein Endlichstes zu wissen!
Welt ist Traum und Traum wird Welt.

There is still a final thing to know! The world is a dream, and the dream will become the world.

Letzte Sehnsucht

Thomas Bernhard (1931-89)

Das Leben ist eine Tortur...
Andererseits kommen wir
Gerade in den Angstzuständen
Zu uns selbst.

Life is torture... On the other hand, we get to know ourselves only when we are in a state of panic.

Die Jagdgesellschaft

Martinus von Biberach (died 1498)

Ich leb und weiß nit wie lang,
Ich stirb und weiß nit wann,
Ich fahr und weiß nit wohin,
Mich wundert, deß ich fröhlich bin.

I am alive, but don't know for how long; I will die, but don't know when; I am travelling, but don't know whither; I am surprised that I am still happy.

Ich leb und weiß nit wie lang

Wolf Biermann (born 1936)

Die Zeit hat ungeheuren Schwung
Paar Jahre bist du stark und jung
Dann sackst du langsam auf den Grund
Der Weltgeschichte.

Time has a tremendous momentum; you are strong
and young for a few years, and then you sag slowly on
to the ground of the world's history.

   Bilanzballade im dreißigsten Jahr

Soldaten sehn sich alle gleich
Lebendig und als Leich.

Soldiers always resemble each other: whether they are
alive or whether they are corpses.

   Soldat, Soldat

Otto von Bismarck (1815-98)

Der alte Jude, das ist der Mann.

The old Jew, that's the man.

   about Disraeli at the Congress of Berlin

Die Politik ist die Lehre von Möglichen.

Politics is the art of the possible.

Die Politik ist keine Wissenschaft, wie viele der Herren
Professoren sich ein-bilden, sonderneine Kunst.

Politics are not a science, as many professors declare,
but an art.

Ehrlicher Makler.

An honest broker.

Macht geht vor Recht.
Might before right.
> *Attributed by his opponents to Bismarck, who repudiated it*

Nach Canossa gehen wir nicht.
We are not going to Canossa.
> *During the Kulturkampf, meaning that he would not submit*
> *to the Vatican*

Setzen wir Deutschland, sozusagen, in den Sattel! Reiten
wird es schon können.
Let us put Germany in the saddle, so to speak; it
already knows how to ride.
> *11 March 1867, in a speech to the North German*
> *Reichstag*

Sie macht sich nur durch Blut und Eisen.
It can be done only through blood and iron.
> *Speaking to the Prussian House of Deputies, 1886*

Wir Detusche fürchten Gott, aber sonst nichts in der Welt.
Und die Gottesfurcht ist es schon, die uns den Frieden
lieben und pflegen läßt.
We Germans fear God but nothing else in the world,
and it is the fear of God which allows us to love and
cherish peace.
> *February 1888, to the Reichstag*

Gebhard Blücher (1742-1819)
Was für Plündern!
What a city to plunder!
> *A misquotation. He actually said 'Was für Plunder!' What a lot of rubbish.*

Vorwärts!
Forward!
> *The motto and the nickname of Blücher*

Frederich von Bodenstedt (1819-92)
In jades Menschen Gesichte
Steht seine Geschichte,
Sein Haßen und Lieben
Deutlich geschrieben.
One can see their life history in the face of all men: their loves and hates are clearly written there.
> *Liedern des Mirza-Schaffy*

Heinrich Böll (1917-85)
Eine Weltkatastrophe kann zu manchem dienen.Auch dazu, ein Alibi finden vor Gott. Wo warst du, Adam? Ich war im Weltkrieg.
A world catastrophe can be useful for some things, including finding an alibi before God. Where were you, Adam? I was in the world war.
> *Wo warst du, Adam?*
> *quoting Haechel*

Es muß etwas geschehen!
Something must happen!
> *Doktor Murkes gesammeltes Schweigen und andere Satiren*

Dietrich Bonhoeffer (1906-45)
Der Mensch für andere.
The man for others.
> *about Jesus*

Wolfgang Borchert (1921-47)
Man kann doch Menschen nicht für ein leeres Wort sterben lassen!
But we cannot let people die for the sake of an empty word!
> *Draußen vor der Tür*

Mit der Wahrheit hat die Kunst doch nichts zu tun!
Art has got nothing to do with truth!
> *Ibid.*

Mit der Wahrheit ist das wie mit einer stadtbekannten Hure. Jeder kennt sie, aber es ist peinlich, wenn man ihr auf der Straße begegnet.
Truth is similar to a well-known town whore. Everyone knows her, but it is embarrassing when one meets her in the street.
> *Ibid.*

Wer Schnaps hat, ist gerettet!
Whoever has schnaps is saved!
> *Ibid.*

Ludwig Börne (1786-1837)
Besiegen könnt ihr uns, aber täuschen nicht mehr.
You may be able to conquer us, but you can no longer deceive us.
> *Briefe aus Paris*

Minister fallen wie Butterbrote: gewöhn-lich auf die gute Seite.
Ministers fall like buttered bread: usually on their good side.
Aphorismen

Willy Brandt (1913-92)
Die Geschichte kennt kein letztes Wort.
History does not recognise a last word.
Erinnerungen

Jetzt wächst zusammen, was zusammengehort.
Now that which belongs together is growing together.
10 Nov. 1989, on the fall of the Berlin Wall

Wir wollen mehr Demokratie wagen.
We want to risk more democracy.
28 October 1969

Wo Hunger herrscht, kann Friede nicht Bestand haben.
Peace cannot endure where hunger rules.
Erinnerungen

Bertolt Brecht (1898-56)
Alle Kreatur braucht Hilf von allen.
All creatures need the help of everyone.
Von der Kindermörderin, Marie Farrar

Alle rennen nach dem Glück
Das Glück rennt hinterher.
Everyone chases after happiness, but happiness is running after them.
Das Lied von der Ünzulänglichkeit men schlichen Strebens

Alles, was über das Leben auf diesem
Planeten zu sagen ist, könnte man in einem einzigen Satz
von mittlerer Länge sagen.
Everything there is to say about life on this planet
could be said in a single sentence of moderate length.
   Baal

Als ihr Mund verstummte, wurde ihre Stimme gehört.
As her mouth grew silent, one could hear her voice.
   Die heilige Johanna der Schlachthöfe

Andrea: Unglücklich das Land, das keine Helden hat!
Galilei: Nein. Unglücklich das Land, das Helden nötig hat.
Andrea: Unhappy the land that has no heroes!
Galileo: No. Unhappy the land that needs heroes.
   Leben des Galilei

Bestechlichkeit ist unsre einzige Aussicht.
Solangs die gibt, gibts milde Urteilssprüche, und sogar der
Unschuldige kann durchkommen vor Gericht.
Corruption is our only hope.As long as we have that
there will be lenient sentences and even the innocent
will survive a trial.
   Mutter Courage und ihre Kinder

Denn ein Haifisch ist kein Haifisch,
Wenn man's nicht beweisen kann.
For a shark is not a shark if it cannot be proved.
   Die Dreigroschenoper

Den für dieses Leben
Ist der Mensch nicht schlau genug.
Man is not crafty enough for this life.
Das Lied von der Unzulänglichkeit menschlichen Strebens
Der Krieg findet immer einen Ausweg.
War always finds a way.
    Mutter Courage und ihre Kinder

Erst kommt das Fressen, dann kommt die Moral.
Food comes first, then morals.
    Die Dreigroschenoper

Es gibt Leute, die ihre Nase in gar alle Angelegenheiten
hineinstecken müssen. Wenn man solchen Leuten den
kleinen Fingerreicht, nehmen sie gleich die ganze Hand.
There are people who have to stick their noses into
absolutely everything. If you reach out your little
finger to such people, they will take your whole hand.
    Mann ist Mann

Gottseidank geht alles schnell vorüber
Auch die Liebe und der Kummer sogar.
Everything passes quickly, thank God – even love and
sorrow.
    Nannas Lied

In den Asphaltstädten bin ich daheim.
I am at home in the asphalt cities.
    Vom armen B.B.

Ist es dem Land nicht egal, wer auf dem Apfelschimmel
sitzt, der es staubig stampft?
Does the land really care who sits on the dapple-grey
horse which paws dustily at it?

Die heilige Johanna derSchlachthöfe

Ohne Beweis ist der Mensch überhaupt kein Mensch,
sondern ein Orang.
Without proof man is actually no man, but an ape.

Elephantenkalb

Sagen Sie mir nicht, daß Friede ausgebrochen ist, wo ich
eben neue Vorräte eingekauft hab.
Don't tell me peace has broken out just when I have
bought new supplies.

Mutter Courage und ihre Kinder

Und der Haifisch, der hat Zähne
Und er tragt sie im Gesicht
Und Macheath, der hat ein Messer
Doch das Messer sicht man nicht.
Oh, the shark has pretty teeth, dear,
And he shows them pearly white.
Just a jackknife has Macheath, dear,
And he keeps it out of sight.

Die Dreigroschenoper

Und weil der Mensch ein Mensch ist, drum will er was zu
essen, bitte sehr!
And because man is a man, he would like something
to eat, please!

Einheitsfrontlied, Svendborger Gedichte

13

Von diesen Städten wird bleiben:der durch sie hindurchging,
der Wind!
All that remains of these cities will be the wind that
blew through them.
   Vom armen B.B.

Weil ich ihm nicht trau, wir sind befreundet.
Because I don't trust him, we are friends.
   Mutter Courage und ihre Kinder

Wer dunkel ist, bleibe dunkel, wer
Unrein ist, unrein. Lobet
Mangel, lobet Mißhandlung, lobet
Die Finsternis.
Whoever is gloomy, stay gloomy, whoever is unclean,
remain unclean. Praise shortcomings, praise ill
treatment, praise the darkness.
   Leben Eduards des Zweiten von England

Wie anstrengend es ist, böse zu sein!
How demanding it is to be wicked!
   Die Maske des Bösen

Will vom Krieg leben
Wird ihm whol müssen auch etwas geben.
He who would live off war must eventually give
something to it.
   Mutter Courage und ihre Kinder

Wir stehen selbst enttäuscht und sehn betroffen
Den Vorhang zu und alle Fragen offen.

...Verehrtes Publikum, los, such dir selbst den Schluß!
Es muß ein gutter da sein, muß, muß, muß!
We stand there in disappointment and look in
consternation at the closed stage curtain that leaves all
questions open... Honoured audience, go, find your
own conclusion! There must be a good one, there
must, there must, there must!

    Der gute Mensch von Sezuan

Georg Büchner (1813-37)

Abe rich, wär ich sehen Sie, ich könnte das Leiden nicht
ertragen - ich würde retten, retten!
But if I were omnipotent, you see, I would not be able
to bear the suffering – I would save, save!

    Woyzeck

Das Leben der Reichen ist ein langer Sonntag.
The life of rich people is one long Sunday.

Das leiseste Zucken des Schmerzes, und rege es sich nur in
einem Atom, macht einen Riß in der Schöpfung von oben
bis unten.
The faintest twinge of pain, even if only in an atom,
creates a fissure in creation from top to bottom.

    Dantons Tod

Der Haß ist so gut erlaubt als die Liebe, und ich hege ihn
im vollsten Maße gegen die, welche ihn verachten.
Hatred is just as allowable as love, and I harbour it in
the fullest measure against those who scorn it.

    Letter to his family, February 1824

Die Guillotine ist der beste Arzt!
The guillotine is the best doctor!
   Dantons Tod

Die Revolution ist wie Saturn, sie frißt ihre eignen Kinder.
The [French] Revolution is like Saturn – it devours its
own children.
   Ibid.

Die Statue der Freiheit ist noch nicht gegossen, der Ofen
glüht, wir alle können uns noch die Finger dabei
Verbrennen.
The Statue of Liberty has not yet been cast. The oven
is glowing and we could still burn our fingers on it.
   Ibid.

Die Sünde ist im Gedanken. Ob der Gedanke Tat wird, ob
ihn der Körper nachspielt, das ist Zufall.
Sin is in the thought. It is a matter of chance if the
thought becomes a deed, if the body acts it out.
   Ibid.

Friede den Hütten! Krieg den Palästen!
Peace to the shacks! War on the palaces!
   Der Hessische Landbote

Ich brauche Thau und Nachtluft wie die Blumen.
Like flowers, I need dew and night air.
   Leonce und Lena

*Ich studierte die Geschichte der Revolution. Ich fühlte mich
wie zernichtet unter dem gräßlichen Fatalismus der
Geschichte.*
I studied the history of the revolution. I felt as if I had
been destroyed by the abominable fatalism of history.
  Letter to Minna Jaegle, 10 March 1834

Ich weiß nicht, was in mir das andere belügt.
I do not know what it is inside me that lies to the
other part.
  Dantons Tod

*Jeder Mensch ist ein Abgrund; es schwindelt einem, wenn
man hinabsieht.*
Every man is a chasm into which it makes one dizzy to
look down.
  Woyzeck

Nur die Toten kommen nicht wieder.
Only the dead never return.
  Dantons Tod

*Wir haben der Schmerzen nicht zu viel, wir haben ihrer zu
wenig, denn durch den Schmerz gehen wir zu Gott ein!*
We do not have too much pain, but too little, for it is
through pain that we attain God.
  On his death bed

17

Prince Bernhard von Bülow (1849-1929)

Mit einem Worte: wir wollen niemand in den Schatten stellen, aber wir verlangen auch unseren Platz an der Sonne.

In a word, we desire to throw no one into the shade [in East Asia], but we also demand our own place in the sun.

To the Reichstag, 6 December 1897

Wilhelm Busch (1832-1908)

Aber hier, wie überhaupt, kommt es anders, als man glaubt.

But in this situation, as usual, it will turn out differently from what one expects.

Plisch und Plum

Dieses war der erste Streich,
Doch der zweite folgt sogleich.

This was the first prank, but the second will follow immediately.

Max und Moritz

Ein Onkel, der Gutes mitbringt, ist besser als eine Tante, die bloß Klavier spielt.

An uncle who brings nice things with him is better than an aunt who only plays the piano.

Aphorismen und Reime

Vater werden ist nicht schwer,
Vater sein dagegen sehr.

Becoming a father is not difficult; being a father, on the other hand, is very hard.

Julchen

Christina Busta (1915-87)

Herr, ich kann nicht mehr beten!
Ich bin müde vom Elend des Menschen,
Vom Leiden der Kreatur.
Deine Schöpfung ist herrlich,
Aber erbarmungslos.

Lord, I can pray no longer. I am tired of the misery of mankind, and of the suffering of creation. Your creation is marvellous, but merciless.

   Salzgärten

Elias Canetti (1905-94)

Alles Wissen hat etwas Puritanisches; es gibt den Worten ein Moral.

All knowledge is somehow puritanical – it gives words a moral.

   Aufzeichnungen

Der Erfolgreiche hört nur noch
Händeklatschen. Sonst ist er taub.

The successful person hears only applause – he is deaf to all else.

   Ibid.

Der Mensch hat die Weisheit all seiner Vorfahren zusammengenommen, und seht, welch ein Dummkopf er ist!

Man has assimilated the collective wisdom of all his ancestors, and see, what a fool he is!

   Ibid.

Der Wind, das einzige Freie in der Zivilisation.
The wind is the only free thing in civilization.
    Aufzeichnungen

*Die meisten Philosophen haben eine zu geringe Vorstellung
von der Variabilität menschlicher Sitten und Möglichkeiten.*
Most philosophers have too narrow a conception of
the variability of human customs and potential.
    Ibid.

*Die Sternbilder waren als Ratschläge gedacht, doch
niemand hat sie verstanden.*
The constellations were considered as a source of
advice, but no one could understand them.
    Ibid.

*Feig, wirklich feig ist nur, wer sich vor seinen Erinnerungen
fürchtet.*
The only person who is truly cowardly is he who is
afraid of his own memories.
    Ibid.

Haben die Tiere weniger Angst, weil sie ohne Worte leben?
Are animals less afraid because they live without
words?
    Ibid.

Immer zierlicher die Uhren, immer gefärlicher die Zeit.
The more delicate the clocks, the more dangerous is
time.
    Ibid.

In der Ewigkeit ist alles am Anfang, duftender Morgen.
In eternity everything is just beginning, a sweet-
scented fragrant morning.
  Aufzeichnungen

Jede Sprache hat ihr eigenes Schweigen.
Every language has its own silence.
  Ibid.

Jeder Krieg enthält alle früheren
Every war contains all earlier wars within it.
  Ibid. (1951)

Musik, das Hohlmaß des Menschen.
Music is the measure of humanity.
  Ibid. (1956)

*Nur das Unerwartete macht glücklich, aber es muß auf viel
Erwartetes stoßen, das es zerstreut.*
Only the unexpected brings happiness, but it must
push against much that is expected and scatter it.
  Ibid.

*Sein Geld hebt er in seinem Herzen auf,
die Schläge zählen es.*
He captures his money in his heart, and his
heartbeats count it.
  Ibid.

Paul Celan (1920-70)
An den langen Tischen der Zeit
Zechen die Krüge Gottes.
The tankards of God make merry at the long table of time.
  Die Krüge

Der Tod ist ein Meister aus Deutschland.
Death is a master from Germany.
  Todesfuge

Die Doggen der Wortnacht.
The mastiffs of the night of words.
  Abend der Worte

Mache mich bitter.
Zähle mich zu den Mandeln.
Make me bitter. Include me among the almonds.
  Zähle die Mandeln

Helmina von Chézy (1783-1856)
Ach, wie ist's möglich dann, daß ich dich lassen kann.
How is it possible that I could leave you?
  Revision of a folk song from the Thüringer Wald

Matthias Claudius (1740-1815)
Ach, sie haben einen guten Mann begraben.
O, they have buried a good man.
  Bei dem Grabe meines Vaters

Greif nicht in ein Wespennast;
Doch wenn du greifst, so stehe fest.
Do not reach into a wasps' nest; but if you do, stand
firm.

    Ein gulden ABC

Karl von Clausewitz (1780-1831)
Der Krieg ist nichts als eine Fortsetzung des politischen
Verkehrs mit Einmischung anderer Mittel.
War is nothing else but a continuation of politics with
an admixture of other means.

Fritz Dietrich (1905-45)
Die großen Tage stehn, bedeckt vom Staube,
Verweilend, breit und still im ebnen Land.
In ihren heißen Händen reift die Traube,
Vergilbt das Feld, verbrennt das Gartenland.
The long days linger, covered in dust, standing wide
and still in the flat land. Their hot hands ripen the
grape, gild the field and scorch the gardens.

    Heißer Sommer

Annette von Droste-Hülshoff (1797-1848)
Herr, ich bin ein arm und kaum noch glühend
Döchtlein am Altare deiner Gnade.
Lord, at the altar of your mercy I am but the poor,
small wick of a candle which scarcely still glows.

    Das geistliche Jahr

Günter Eich (1907-72)

Wer möchte ohne den Trost der Bäume leben?

Who would want to live without the consolation of the trees.

Ende eines Sommers

Wo ist er nun, der große Traum der Erde, Der Traum von Vogelflug und Pflanzensein? Die Dinge bleiben doch, ihr altes Werde, Ihr alter Tod und ach, altes Nein.

Where is it now, the great dream of the earth, the dream of the flight of birds and the existence of plants? Things remain, with their ancient development, their ancient death, and oh, their ancient denial.

Märztag

Joseph von Eichendorff (1788-1857)

Die Luft ging durch die Felder,
Die Ähren wogten sacht,
Es rauschten leis die Wälder,
So sternklarwar die Nacht.

The breeze blew through the fields, the ears of corn undulated gently, the woods rustled quietly, so starry clear was the night.

Mondnacht

Albert Einstein (1879-1955)

Jedenfalls bin ich uberzeugt, daß der nicht würfelt.

Anyway I am convinced that He [God] does not play dice.

Friedrich Engels (1820-95)
Der Staat wird nicht 'abgeschafft', er stirbt ab.
The State is not 'abolished', it withers away.

Die Geschichte aller bisherigen Gesellschaft ist die
Geschichte von Klassenkämpfen.
The history of all previous society is the history of
class war.
   Manifest der Kommunistischen Partei (with Karl Marx)

Die Proletarier haben nichts zu verlieren als ihre Ketten.
The proletariat have nothing to lose except their
chains.
   Ibid.

Ein Gespenst geht um in Europa – das Gespenst des
Kommunismus.
A spectre is haunting Europe – the spectre of
communism.
   Ibid.

August Heinrich Hoffmann von Fallersleben (1798-1874)
Der größte Lump im ganzen Land, das ist und bleibt der
Denunziant.
The greatest rogue in the whole land is, and will
remain, the informer.
   Politische Gedichte aus der deutschen Vorzeit

Deutschland, Deutschland über alles.
Germany, Germany, above everything else.
   Das Lied der Deutschen

Und wir müssen wandern, wandern,
Keiner weiß vom andern.
And we must wander, wander, no one being aware of
the other's existence.

   Niemals wieder

Proletarier aller Länder, vereinigt euch!
Workers of the world, unite!

   Ibid.

Kurt Feltz (1910-82)
Es geht alles vorüber,
Es geht alles vorbei,
Auf jeden Dezember
Folgt wieder ein Mai.
Everything passes, everything ends, a May always
follows every December.

   Es geht alles vorüber

Ludwig Feuerbach (1804-72)
Der Mensch ist, was er ißt.
Man is what he eats.

Cäsar Flaischlen (1864-1920)
Hab Sonne im Harzen ob's stürmt oder schneit,
ob der Himmel voll Wolken, die erde voll Streit!
Carry the sun in your heart even if it is stormy or
snowing, if the sky is cloudy or the earth resounds
with strife.

   Aus den Lehr-und Wanderjahren des Lebens

Theodor Fontane (1819-98)
Courage ist gut, aber Ausdauer ist besser.
Courage is good, but endurance is better.

Man darf Heldentaten nicht in der Nähe betrachten.
One should not examine heroic deeds closely.
Ein Sommer in Londen

Man hat's, oder man hat's nicht.
One either has it, or one doesn't.
Man hat es oder man hat es nicht

Kaiser Friedrich III (1831-88)
Lerne leiden, ohne zu klagen, das ist das einzige, was ich dich lehren kann.
Learn to suffer without complaint; this is the only thing I can teach you.
Advice to his son

Frederick the Great (1712-86)
Ich bin es müde, über Sklaven zu herrschen.
I am tired of ruling slaves.
To his cabinet, c.1786

Ihr Racker, wollt ihr ewig leben?
Rascals, would you live forever?
To his hesitant troops

Jeder muß nach seiner Fasson selig werden.
Everyone must find his own salvation.

Erich Fried (1921-88)

Ich habe meine Lehrzeit
Hinter mir.
My apprenticeship is behind me.
   Fast Alles

Max Frisch (1911-91)

Einmal werd ich die Wahrheit sagen-das meint man, aber
die Lüge ist ein Egel, sie hat die Wahrheit ausgesaugt.
One day I shall tell the truth – that is what one thinks,
but the lie is a leech and has sucked the truth dry.
   Andorra

Alfred Funke (1869- ?)

Gott strafe England!
God punish England!

Salomon Gessner (1730-88)

Wenn deine Schrift dem Kenner nichtgefällt
So ist es schon ein böses Zeichen:
Doch wenn sie gar des Narren Lob erhalt
So ist es Zeit, sie auszustreichen.
When your writings fail to please knowledgeable
critics, that is certainly a bad sign: but when they are
praised by fools, it is time to expunge them.

Christian Fürchtegott Gellert (1715-69)

Er ward geboren,
Er lebte, nahm ein Weib und starb.
He was born, he lived, took a wife, and died.
   Der Greis

Ja, ja, Prozeße müßen sein.
Yes, yes, there must be trials.
   Der Prozeß

Hans-Dietrich Genscher (born 1927)
Die Presse ist die Artillerie der Freiheit.
The press is the artillery of freedom.

Günter Grass (born 1927)
Getauft geimpft gefirmt geschult.
Gespielt hab ich mit Bombensplittern
Und aufgewachsen bin ich zwischen Dem
Heiligen Geist und Hitlers Bild.
Baptised, vaccinated, confirmed, educated, I played
with fragments of bombs and grew up between the
Holy Spirit and Hitler's portrait.
   Kleckerburg

Joseph Goebbels (1897-1945)
Ohne Butter warden wir fertig, ohne nicht beispielsweise
ohne Kanonen. Wenn wir einmal überfallen warden, dann
können wir uns nicht mit Butter, sondern nur mit Kanonen
verteidigen.
We can manage without butter, but not, for example,
without guns. If we are attacked we cannot defend
ourselves with butter, only with guns.

Vor diesem einschließlich der Sowjetunion riesigen
Territorium würde sich sofort ein eiserner Vorhang
heruntersenken.
An iron curtain would at once descend on this

territory which, including the Soviet Union, would be of gigantic size.

In 1945, on the consequences if Germany were to surrender

Wie selig lebt ein Mann, der seine Pflichten kennt!
How blessed is the man who knows his duty!

Der Menschenfreund

Johann Wolfgang von Goethe (1748-1837)

Ach, daß die Einfalt, daß die Unschuld nie
Sich selbst und ihren heil'gen Wert erkennt!
Oh, that simplicity and innocence never recognise themselves and their sacred value!

Faust

Ach, ich bin des Treibens müde!
O, I am tired of the struggle.

Wandrers Nachtlied

Allah braucht nicht mehr zu schaffen,
Wir erschaffen seine Welt.
Allah need no longer create: we are creating his world.

Wiederfinden

Alles in der Welt läßt sich ertragen, nur nicht eine Reihe von schönen Tagen.
Everything in the world is bearable, except a series of lovely days.

Gedichtsammlung, 1815

Am Ende hängen wir doch ab
Von Kreaturen, die wir machten.
In the end we remain dependent on creatures of our
own making.

    Faust

Am Jüngsten Tag, wenn die Posaunen schallen,
Und alles aus ist mit dem Erdeleben,
Sind wir verpflichtet Rechenschaft zu geben
Von jedem Wort, das unnütz uns entfallen.
On the Day of Judgement, when the trumpets sound
and earthly life is finished, we shall have to account
for every idle word that has fallen from our lips.

    Warnung

Bezähme jeder die gerechte Wut
Und spare für das Ganze seine Rache:
Denn Raub begeht am allgemeinenen Gut,
Wer selbst sich hilft in seiner eignen Sache.
Everyone should control his righteous anger and save his
revenge for the whole. For whoever helps himself robs
the common good.

    Werke

Blut ist ein ganz besondrer Saft.
Blood is a very special juice.

    Faust

Da wo wir lieben,
Ist Vaterland;
Wo wir genießen
Ist Hof und Haus.
The place that we love is the fatherland; the places in which we enjoy ourselves are the garden and home.
   Felsweihegesang an Psyche

Dahin! Dahin geht unser Weg!
There! There goes our way!
   Wilhelm Meisters Lehjahre

Das Ewig-Weibliche
Zieht uns hinan.
The eternal feminine draws us upwards.
   Faust

Das Haß ist parteiisch, aber die Liebe ist es noch mehr.
Hate is unfair, but love even more so.

Der Aberglaube ist die Poesie des Lebens.
Superstition is the poetry of life.

Der Druck der Geschäfte ist schön der Seele; wenn sie
entladen ist, spielt sie freier und genieß des Lebens.
Business pressures are good for the soul; when it has unburdened itself of them, it plays all the more freely and enjoys life.
   Tagebuch

Der du die weite Welt umschweiffst, geschäftiger Geist, wie
nah fühl ich mich dir.
You who wander the wide world, busy spirit, how close I
feel to you.

   Faust

Der früh Geliebte,
Nicht mehr Getrübte,
Er kommt zurück!
The beloved of long ago, no more befogged, is coming
back!

   Ibid.

Der Glaube ist wie die Liebe: er läßt sich nicht erzwingen.
Faith is like love: neither can be forced.

Der hohe Sinn des Papsts,
Er sieht das Kleine klein, das Grosse gross.
The lofty mind of the Pope, who sees what is small as
small, and what is great as great.

   Torquato Tasso

Der kann sich manchen Wunsch gewähren, Der kalt sich
selbst und seinem Willen lebt; Allein wer andre wohl zu
leiten strebt, Muß fähig sein, viel zu entbehren.
He who lives coldly and according to his will can grant
his own wishes; but he who strives to lead others
must be capable of many sacrifices.

   Ilmenau

Der Kopf steht mir wie eine Wetterfahne, wenn ein Gewitter heraufzieht und die Windstöße veränderlich sind.
My head feels like a weathervane when a thunderstorm is approaching and the gusts of wind are changeable.
  Letter to J.D. Salzmann, 1771

Der Leichnam ist nicht das ganze Tier.
The body is not the entire animal.
  Letter to Herr Hetzler, 1770

Der Mensch ist doch wie ein Nachtgänger; er steigt die gefährlichsten Kanten im Schlafe.
Man is like a sleepwalker; he climbs dangerous ledges in his sleep.
  Letter to Charlotte von Stein, 1780

Der Umgang mit Frauen ist das Element gutter Sitten.
The company of women is the school of good manners.

Der Zufall wohl pathetische, niemals aber tragische Situationen her-vorbringen dürfe; das Schicksal hingegen muße immer fürchterlich sein.
Chance may create pathetic, but never tragic, situations; fate, on the other hand, must always be awesome.
  Wilhelm Meisters Lehrjahre

Der Zweck des Lebens ist das Leben selbst.
The purpose of life is life itself.

Des Menschen Leben ist ein ähnliches Gedicht:
Es hat wohl einen Anfang, hat ein Ende,
Allein ein Ganzes ist es nicht.
Human life resembles a poem: it certainly has a
beginning and an end; but it is not complete.
  Faust

Die Menschen sin dim ganzen Leben blind.
Men are blind throughout their entire lives.
  Ibid.

Die Nachahmung ist uns angeboren, das
Nachzuahmende wird nicht leicht erkannt.
Imitation is natural to us, but it is not easy to
recognise what should be imitated.
  Wilhelm Meisters Lehrjahre

Die Unruhe und Ungewissenheit sind unser Theil.
Unrest and uncertainty are our lot.
  Letter to Sophie von La Roche, 1774

Die Wahlverwandtschaften.
Elective affinities.
  Title of a book

Die Zeit wird Herr
Time will become master.
  Faust

Doch alles, was dazu mich tribe
Gott, war so gut! ach, war so lieb!
But everything that drove me to it, God, was so good,
so lovely!

    Faust

Du bleibst doch immer, was du bist.
You will always remain what you are.

    Ibid.

Du danke Gott, wenn er dich preßt,
Und dank' ihm, wenn er dich wieder entläßt.
You should thank God when he oppresses you, and
thank him when he releases you again.

    Gesprächte mit J.P. Eckermann

Du mußt herrschen und gewinnen,
Oder dienen und verlieren,
Leiden oder triumphieren
Amboß oder Hammer sein.
One must be master and win or serve and lose, grieve
or triumph, be the anvil or the hammer.

    Der Groß-Cophta

Du sprichst ein großes Wort gelassen aus.
Calmly you speak a momentous word.

Du wohnst bei mir Urquell der Natur,
Leben und Freude der Creatur.
You live within me, primal fountain of nature, life and
joy of creation.

    Des Künstlers Erdewallen

Durch zweier Zeugen Mund
Wird allerwegs die Wahrheit kund.
Truth is established everywhere from the mouths of two
witnesses.

   Faust

Eigentlich weiß man nur, wenn man wenig weiß; mit dem
Wissen wächst der Zweifel.
One is knowledgeable only when one knows little;
doubt grows with knowledge.

   Maximen und Relexionen

Ein Blick von dir, ein Wort, mehr unterhält Als alle
Weisheit dieser Welt.
One of your glances, one word, says more than all the
wisdom in this world.

   Faust

Ein echter deutscher Mann mag keinen Franzen leiden,
Doch ihre Weine trinkt er gern.
A true German cannot bear the French, but he enjoys
drinking their wine.

   Ibid.

Ein Mächtiger, der für die Seinen nicht
Zu sorgen weiss, wird von dem Volke Selbst Getadelt.
A man of power who cannot look after the interests of
his own favourites will be blamed eevn by the general
public.

   Torquato Tasso

Entbehren sollst Du! Sollst entbehren! Das ist der ewige
Gesang.
Deny yourself! You must deny yourself! That is the
eternal song.
  Ibid.

Er nennt's Vernunft und braucht's allein, Nur tierischer als
jedes Tier zu sein.
He calls it reason but only uses it to be more bestial than
any beast
  Ibid.

Es bildet ein Talent sich in der Stille
Sich ein Charakter in dem Strom der Welt.
Talent is shaped in tranquility, character in the stream
of life.
  Torquato Tasso

Es irrt der Mensch, so lang er strebt.
Man will err as long as he strives.
  Faust

Es war getan, fast eh' gedacht.
It was done almost as soon as it was conceived of.
  Willkommen und Abschied

Folgte Begierde dem Blick, folgte Genuß der Begier.
Desire followed a glance, and pleasure followed desire.
  Römische Elegien

Füllest wieder Busch und Tal
Still mit Nebelglanz,
Lösest endlich auch einmal
Meine Seele ganz.
You quietly fill thickets once more and valleys with the gleam of fog, and also finally and completely release my soul.

  An den Mond

Geburt und Grab, ein ewiges Meer.
Birth and the grave, an eternal sea.

  Faust

Gefühl ist alles:
Name ist Schall und Rauch,
Umnebelnd Himmelsglut.
Feeling is everything: a name is but the sound and smoke that cloud the heavenly fire.

  Ibid.

Geschichte schreiben ist eine Art, sich das Vergangene vom Halse zu schaffen.
Writing history is a way of getting rid of the past which hangs around one's neck.

  Maximen und Reflexionen

Gib meine Jugend mir zurück!
Give me back my youth.

  Faust

Gott hat den Menschen einfach gemacht, aber wie er gewickelt und sich verwickelt ist schwer zu sagen.
God made man simple. How he evolved and became complicated is hard to say.
  Letter to Charlotte von Stein, 11 December 1778

Grau, teurer Freund, ist alle Theorie, Und grün des Lebens goldner Baum.
Grey my dearest friend, is the colour of all theory, and green is the colour of the golden tree of life.
  Faust

Hätte Gott mich anders gewollt, so hätt' er mich anders gemacht.
If God had wanted me to be different, he would have created me differently.

Hätte ich nicht die Welt durch Anticipation bereits in mir getragen, ich ware mit sehen den Augen blind geblieben.
If I had not already borne the world within me through anticipation, despite my seeing eyes I would have remained blind.
  Letter to J.P .Eckermann, 26 February 1824

Heilige Gluten!
Wen sie umschweben,
Fühlt sich im Leben
Selig mit Gutem
Sacred fires! He around whom they hover feels his life blessed with goodness.
  Faust

Höchstes Glück der Erdenkinder
Sei nur die Persönlichkeit.
The highest fortune of earth's children is seen in
personality alone.
   West-östliche Divan

Ich bin der Geist, der stets verneint.
I am the spirit that always says no.
   Faust (the reply of Mephistopheles when asked his name)

Ich bin nun wie ich bin;
So nimm mich nur hin!
I am what I am, so accept me as such!
   Liebhaber in allen Gestalten

Ich bin wie immer bald leidlich bald unleidlich.
As always, I am reasonable one moment, unreasonable
the next.
   Letter to Johanna Fahlmer, 31 October 1773

Ich seh sie dort, ich she sie hier
Und weiß nicht auf der Welt,
Und wie und wo und wann sie mir
Warum sie mir gefällt.
I see her here, I see her there, and do not know why
in the world, how, where, and when, she appeals to
me.
   Auf Christiane R

In der Kunst ist das Beste gut genug.
In art the best is good enough.

Je mehr du fühlst, ein Mensch zu sein,
Desto ähnlicher bist du den Göttern!
The more you feel yourself to be human, the more you resemble the gods!

   Zahme Xenien

Jeder glaubt,
Es sei auch schicklich, was ihm nützlich ist.
Everyone believes that what is useful to him is also proper.

   Torquato Tasso

Jeder Mensch ist ein Adam; denn jeder wird einmal aus
dem Paradiese der warmen Gefühle vertrieben.
Every man is an Adam, for everybody is one day driven out of the paradise of warm feelings.

   Letter to J.C. Lobe, July 1820

Jugend ist Trunkenheit ohne Wein.
Youth is drunkenness without wine.

   Westöstliche Diwan, 'Schenkenbuch'

Kein lebendiges ist ein Eins,
Immer ist's ein Vieles.
No living creature is a single thing, it is always a multiple.

   Epirrhema

Kennst Du das Land, wo die Zitronen blühn?
Im dunkelm Laub die Gold-Orangen glühn,
Ein sanfter Wind vom blauen Himmel weht,
Die Myrte still und hoch der Lorbeer steht –

Kennst due s wohl? Dahin! Dahin
Möcht' ich mit dir, o mein Geliebter, ziehn!
Do you know the country where the lemons bloom?
Among the dark leaves the golden oranges glow, a soft
wind wafts from the blue sky, the myrtle is still and the
laurel stands high-do you know it well? There, there,
would I go, oh my beloved, with thee.

Wilhelm Meisters Lehjahre

Mags schnell geschehn, was muß geschehn!
Let that which must happen happen quickly!

Faust

Mehr Licht!
More light!

Dying

Mein armer Kopf
Ist mir verrückt,
Mein armer Sinn
Ist mir zerstückt.
My poor head is in disarray, my poor mind is breaking
up.

Faust

Mein Kind, ich hab' es klug gemacht:
Ich habe nie über das Denken gedacht.
My child I have behaved very cleverly – I have never
thought about thinking.

Zahme Xenien

Meine Ruh' ist hin,
Mein Herz ist schwer.
My peace is gone, my heart is heavy.
   Faust

Neugier nur beflügelt jeden Schritt.
Curiosity alone inspires every step.
   Ibid.

Niemand ist mehr Sklave, als der sich für frei hält, ohne es
zu sein.
No one is more truly a slave than he who thinks
himself free without being so.

Nur rastlos betätigt sich der Mann.
Man acts only through restlessness.
   Faust

Ob er heilig, ob er böse,
Jammert sie den Unglücksmann.
Whether he's holy or evil, this unlucky man is pitied.
   Ibid.

Oh, wär' ich nie geboren!
Oh, if only I had never been born!
   Ibid.

Ohne Hast, aber ohne Rast.
Without haste but without pause.
   Zahme Xenien

Poesie und Wissenschaft erscheinen als die größten
Widersacher.
Poetry and science appear the greatest adversaries
   Zur Morphologie

Selig wer sich vor der Welt
Ohne Haß verschließt.
Blessed is he who can shut himself off from the world
without hating it.
   Der Mondlied

Selten wird das Treffliche gefunden, seltner geschätzt.
Excellence is rarely found; even more rarely is it valued.
   Wilhelm Meisters Lehrjahre

So lang man lebt, sei man lebendig!
As long as we live, let us be alive!
   Maskenzug

So tauml' ich von Begierde zu Genuß,
Und im Genuß versvhmacht' ich nach Begierde.
I stagger thus from desire to enjoyment, and in
enjoyment I languish for desire.
   Faust

Staub soll er fressen, und mit Lust.
He shall gobble dust and enjoy it.
   Ibid.

Stirb und werde!
Die and become!
   Selige Sehnsucht

Tu nur das Rechte in deinen Sachen; das andre wird sich
von selber machen.
Make sure that you only do the right thing in life;
everything else will take care of itself.
   Gedichtsammlung, 1815

Über allen Gipfeln ist Ruh'.
Over all the mountain tops is peace.
   Wanderers Nachtliled

Überlegung ist eine Kranckheit der Seele, und hat nur
krancke Taten getan.
Reflection is a disease of the soul, and has performed
only sick deeds.
   Götz von Berlichingen (first version)

Und doch, welch Glück, geliebt zu warden!
Und lieben, Götter, Welch ein Glück!
And even so, what happiness to be loved! And, oh
you gods, what happiness it is to love!
   Willkommen und Abschied

Und was der ganzen Menschheit zugeteilt ist,
Will ich in meinem inner Selbst genießen.
I want to savour in my inner self that which is granted
to the whole of mankind.
   Urfaust

Von der Gewalt, die alle Wesen bindet Befreit der Mensch

sich, der sich überwindet.
He who masters himself is freed from the force which
binds all creatures.
  Die Geheimnisse

Von hier und heute geht eine neue Epoche der Welt-
geschichte aus, und ihr könnt sagen, ihr seid dabeigewesen.
Here and today begins a new era in world history, and
you can say that you were there.
  19 September 1792, on the eve of the barrage of Valmy

Was einem angehört, wiord man nicht los, und wenn man
es wegwürfe.
One cannot get rid of that which belongs to one, even
if one throws it away.
  Maximen und Reflexionen

Was glänzt, ist für den Augenblick geboren.
A thing that glitters is made only for the moment.

Was soll all der Schmerz und Lust?
Süßer Friede,
Komm, ach komm in meine Brust!
Why all the pain and pleasure? Sweet peace, enter, oh
enter, my breast!
  Wanderers Nachtlied

Wenn ich nicht sinnen oder dichten soll,
So ist das Leben mir keinen Leben mehr.
If I may not ponder or write, then life is no longer any
sort of life for me.
  Torquato Tasso

Wer immer strebend sich bemüht
Den können erlösen.
We can rescue him who constantly strives.
   Faust

Wer lange lebt, hat viel erfahren,
Nichts kann für ihn auf dieser Welt geschehn.
He who has lived for a long time has experienced
much. For him, nothing new can happen in this
world.
   Ibid.

Wer nie sein Brot mit Tränen aß,
Wer nie die kummervollen Nächte
Auf seinem Bette weinend saß,
Der Kennt euch nicht, ihr himmlischen Mächte.
Who never ate his bread with tears nor spent a
mournful night upon his bed knows you not, you
heavenly powers.
   Wilhelm Meisters Lehjahre

Wer reitet so spat durch Nacht und Wind?
Who rides so late throught the night and the wind?
   Der Erlkönig

Wüchsen die Kinder in der Art fort, wie sie sich andeuten,
so hätten wir lauter Genies.
If children continued to develop according to their
early indications, we would have nothing but genius.
   Dichtung und Wahrheit

Wunder ist des Glaubens liebstes Kind.
Wonder is belief's favourite child.
   Faust

Zwei Seelen wohnen, ach! in meiner Brust!
Alas! Two souls live within my breast!
   Ibid.

Franz Grillparzer (1791-1872)
Das Edle schwindet von der weiten Erde,
Das Hohe sieht vom Niedern sich verdrängt,
Und Freiheit wird sich nennen die Gemeinheit,
Als Gleichheit brüsten sich der dunkle Neid.
Nobility is fading from the wide world, the lofty sees
itself being driven out by the lowly. Vulgarity will call it
self freedom, and dark envy will boast of itself as
equality.
   Libussa

Der Weg der neueren Bildung geht
Von Humanität
Durch Nationalität
Zur Bestialität.
The path of the new education leads from humanity to
nationality to bestiality.
   Epigram of 1849

Der Zweifel zeugt den Zweifel an sich selbst.
Doubt generates doubt of itself.
   Ein Bruderzwist in Habsburg

Im Haufen steht die Tierwelt gar zu nah.
In crowds of people the animal kingdom seems far too close.

Ein Bruderzwist in Habsburg

Recht ist nur der ausgeschmückte Name Für alles
Unrechte, das die Erde hegt.
Justice is only the decorative name for all the injustice that the world harbours.

Libussa

Und die Große ist gefährlich
Und der Ruhm ein leeres Spiel.
Greatness is dangerous, and glory is an empty game.

Der Traum ein Leben

Unsre Taten sind nur Würfe
In des Zufalls blinder Nacht.
Our deeds are only throws of the dice in the blind night of chance.

Die Ahnfrau

The Brothers Grimm (Wilhelm 1785-1859; Jacob 1786-1836)

Ach, wie gut, daß niemand weiß, daß ich Rumpelstilzchen heißt!
It is just as well that no one knows that my name is Rumpelstiltskin.

Rumpelstilzchen Märchen

Friedrich Halm (1806-71)

Mein Herz ich will dich fragen:
Was ist denn lieber? Sag'!
'Zwei Seelen und ein Gedanke,
Zwei Herzen und ein Schlag!'
What love is, if thou wouldst be taught,
Thy heart must teach alone.
Two souls with but a single thought,
Two hearts that beat as one.

Otto Erich Hartleben (1864-1905)

Die finstern Wolken lagern
Schwer auf dem greisen Land,
Die welken Blätter rascheln,
Was glänzt, ist Herbstes-Tand.
The dark clouds lie heavily over the ancient land; the
wilted leaves rustle, and what gleams are the trinkets
of autumn.
  Trutzlied

Gerhart Hauptmann (1862-1946)

Vor der Kunst wie vor dem Gesetz sind alle Menschen gleich.
All men are equal before art, as before the law.
  Die Ratten

Friedrich von Hausen (c 1150-90)

Gelebte ich noch die lieben zît
Daz ich daz lant solt aber schouwen,
Dar inne al min fröude lît
Nu lange an einer schoenen frouwen.
If only I still lived in that blessed time when I could

see my own country and when all my pleasure lay in a beautiful woman.

Heimweh

Friedrich Hebbel (1813-63)
So weit im Leben, ist zu nah am Tod!
To be advanced in life is to be too close to death!

Sommerbild

Heinrich Heine (1797-1856)
Auf Flügeln des Gesanges.
On wings of song.

title of a song

Das Glück ist eine leichte Dirne,
Sie weilt nicht gern am selben Ort;
Sie streicht das Haar dir aus der Stirne
Und küßt dich rasch und flattert fort.
Good fortune is a loose woman who does not like to tarry in the same place for long; she strokes the hair back from your forehead, kisses you quickly and flutters off.

Romanzero

Den Himmel überlassen wir den Engeln und den Spatzen.
We will leave heaven to the angels and the sparrows.

Deutschland. Ein Wintermärchen

Dort, wo man Bücher verbrennt, verbrennt man am Ende auch Menschen.
Whenever books are burned, in the end men too are burned.

Almansor

Hört ihr das Glockchen klingeln? Kniet nieder – Man
bringt die Sakramente einem sterbenden Gotte.
Do you hear the little bell tinkling? Kneel down. The
sacrament is being brought to a dying god.

Ich habe geliebt manch schönes Kind
Und manchan guten Gasellen.
Wo sind sie hin? Es pfeift der Wind,
Es schäumen und wandern die Wellen.
I have loved many a pretty child, and some good
fellows. Where have they gone? The wind whistles,
and the waves foam and move on.

   Träumen

Ich habe gerochen alle Gerüche
In dieser holden Erdenküche;
Was man genießen kann in der Welt,
Das hab' ich genoßen wie je ein Held!
I have smelled all the aromas there are in this sweet
earthly kitchen; everything that one can enjoyed like a
hero!

   Rückschau

Ich weiß nicht, was soll es bedeuten,
Daß ich so traurig bin;
Ein Märchen aus alten Zeiten,
Das kommt mir nicht aus dem Sinn.
I don't know what it portends that I should feel so
sad. A fairy story from olden times keeps running
through my mind.

   'Die Lorelei', Buch der Lieder

Kein Talent, doch ein Charakter.
No talent, but a character.

Still ist die Nacht, es ruhen die Gassen,
In diesem Hause wohnte mein Schatz;
Sie hat schon längst die Stadt verlassen,
Doch steht noch das Haus auf demselben Platz.
The night is still, the streets are quiet; in this house
my darling lived. Long ago she left this town, but the
house still stands where it used to be.
   Buch der Lieder

Wo wird einst des Wandermüden
Letzte Ruhestätte sein?
Where will the final resting place be for him who is
tired of wandering?
   Wo

Georg Hegel (1770-1831)
Die Wahrheit ist das Ganze.
Truth is the whole.

Es ist der Gang Göttes in der Welt, daß der Staat ist: sein
Grund ist die Gewalt der sich als Wille verwirklichenden
Vernunft.
It is God's way with the world that the State exists,
based on the power of reason which realises itself as
will.
   Grundlinien der Philosophie des Rechts

Für einen Kammerdiener giebt es keinen Held.
No man is a hero to his valet.

Hermann Hesse (1877-1962)
Glauben ist Vertrauen, nicht Wissenwollen.
Belief is trust, not knowledge.
  Lektüre für Minuten

Max Herrmann-Neisse (1889-1932)
Im Lieben und im Haßen
Wie einig waren wir!
Wenn alle dich verlassen,
Kehrst du zurück zu mir!
How united we were in love and in hate! When
everyone deserts you, you will return to me!
  Verlassen

Adolf Hitler (1889-1945)
Brennt Paris?
Is Paris burning?

Das gesamte Leben läßt sich in drei Thesen zusammenfassen:
der Kampf ist der Vater aller Dinge, die Tungend ist eine
Angelegenheit des Bluts, Führertum ist primär entscheidend.
The whole of life can be summed up in three
propositions: struggle is the father of all things; virtue
lies in the blood; leadership is primarily decisiveness.
  Letter to Heinrich Brüning

Das Wort baut Brücken in unerforschte Gebiete.
Words build bridges in unexplored areas.

Der Glaube ist schwerer zu erschüttern als das Wissen.
Belief is harder to shake than knowledge.
  Mein Kampf

Der Kampf hat den Menschen groß gemacht.
Struggle has made mankind great.
   Letter to Heinrich Brüning

Der schwerster Schlag den die Menschheit je erlebte, war die Einführung des Christentum.
The heaviest blow that mankind has ever experienced was the introduction of Christianity.

Die breite Masse eines Volkes fällt einer großen Lüge leichter zum Opfer als einer kleinen.
The broad mass of the people will fall victim to a big lie more easily than a small one.

Die ganze Natur ist ein gewaltiges Ringen zwischen Kraft und Schwäche.
The whole of nature is a mighty struggle between strength and weakness.
   To Heinrich Brüning

Die Idee des Kampfes ist so alt wie das Leben selbst.
The idea of struggle is as old as life itself.

Die Nacht der langen Messer.
The night of the long knives.
   Quoting a Nazi marching song, applied to the killing of Roehm and his colleagues

Ein Mensch, der kein Gefühl für Geschichte hat, ist wie einer ohne Augen und Ohren.
A person who has no feeling for history is like a man who has no eyes and ears.

*Eines kann ich den Fleischessern prophezeien: Die
Gesellschaft der Zukunft wird vegetarisch leben.*
There is one thing that I can predict to the flesh-
eaters: the society of the future will be vegetarian.

*Es gibt nur ein Recht in der Welt, und dieses Recht liegt in
der eigenen Stärke.*
There is only one sort of justice in the world, and that
lies in individual strength.

Munich, 22 September 1928

*Es ist die letzte territoriale Forderung, die ich Europa zu
stellen habe, aber es ist die Forderung, von der ich nicht
abgehe, und die ich, so Gott will, erfüllen werde.*
It is the last territorial claim which I have in Europe,
but it is the claim from which I will not retreat, and
which, God willing, I shall achieve.

About the Sudetenland

*Falsche Begriffe und schlechtes Wissen können durch
Belehrung beseitigt werden.*
False ideas and scanty knowledge can be eliminated
by instruction.

*In Bezug auf das sudetendeutsche Problem meine Gedul
jetzt zu Ende ist!*
With regard to the problem of the Sudeten Germans
my patience is now at an end!

Speech, 26 September 1938

Kraft ist oberstes Gesetz.
Power is the highest law.

Niemand kann sagen, ob die kommende Generation eine Generation von Giganten sein wird.
No one can say whether the coming generation will be a generation of giants.

So wie die Welt nicht von Kriegen lebt, so leben die Völker nicht von Revolutionen.
Just as the world does not live by wars, neither do people live by revolutions.
  Mein Kampf

Wenn ich nicht morgen nachmittag Sieger bin, bin ich ein toter Mann!
If I am not the victor by tomorrow afternoon, I shall be a dead man.
  Munich, 8 November 1923

Wer nicht die Kraft hat, dem nutzt das 'Recht an sich' gar nichts.
Having 'right on one's side' is absolutely useless if one has no power.

Wie klein denken doch kleine Menschen!
What little thoughts are thought by little people!

Wir führen einen Kampf auf Leben und Tod und können zur Zeit keine Geschenke machen.
We are waging a life and death struggle and can make no concessions to time.
  Letter to Franco, 1940

Hugo von Hofmannsthal (1874-1929)
*Ich hab' mich so an Künstliches verloren, Daß ich die
Sonne sah aus toten Augen Und nicht mehr hörte als durch
tote Ohren.*
I had so abandoned myself to artificiality that I saw
the sun with dead eyes, and could no longer hear
except with deaf ears.

    Der Tor und der Tod

*Jedes vollkommene Gedicht ist Ahnung und Gegenwart,
Sehnsucht und Erfüllung zugleich. Gespräch über Gedichte.*
Every perfect poem is simultaneously a premonition
and the present, longing and fulfilment. A conversation
more than a poem.

Friedrich Hölderlin (1770-1843)
Alles Getrennte findet sich wieder.
All that is divided will find itself again.

    Hyperion

Beruf ist mirs, zu rühmen Höhers.
My profession is to praise higher things.

    Die Prinzessin Auguste von Homburg

*Denn, Ihr Deutschen, auch Ihr seid
Tatenarm und gedankenvoll.*
You Germans are also poor in deeds and full of thought.

    An die Deutschen

*Denn schwer ist zu tragen
Das Unglück, aber schwerer das Glück.*
Although misfortune is hard to bear, good fortune is

even harder.
Der Rhein

*Der die dunkle Zukunft sieht, der muß auch sehen den Tod
und allein ihn fürchten.*
He who sees the dark future must also see death, and
fear it alone.
Der Mensch

*Die ewigen Götter sind
Voll Lebens allzeit; bis in den Tod
Kann aber ein Mensch auch
Im Gedächtnis doch das Beste behalten,
Und dann erlebt er das Höchste.*
The eternal gods are always full of life; but a man too
can keep the best in his memory until his death. Then
he will experience the highest things.
Der Rhein

*Doch uns ist gegeben,
Auf keiner Stätte zu ruhn.*
We are fated, however, not to find a resting place.
Hyperioins Schicksalslied

Es ehret der Knecht nur den Gewaltsamen.
Servants honour only the powerful.
Menschenbeifall

Heilige Gefäße sind die Dichter.
Poets are sacred vessels.
Buonaparte

In seiner Fülle ruhet der Herbsttag nun.
Now the autumn day rests amid its rich plenty.
   Mein Eigentum

Hans Egon Holthusen (1913-97)
*Glaube und Zweifel verhalten sich zueinander wie
Regierung und Opposition in einem parlamentarischen
Gemeinwesen.*
Belief and doubt relate to each other in the same way
as government and opposition in a parliament body.
   Verstehen

Arno Holz
Die Kunst hat die Tendenz, wieder die Natur zu sein.
Art has a tendency to revert to nature.
   Die Kunst, ihr Wesen und ihre Gesetze

Hans Johst (1843-1929)
Wenn ich Kultur höre entsichere ich meine Browning.
When I hear the word 'culture', I slip the safety-catch
of my Browning.
   (but usually attributed to Goering)

Carl Jung (1875-1961)
*Ein gewissermaßen oberflächliche Schicht des
Unbewußten ist zweifellos persönlich. Wir nennen sie das
persönliche Unbewußte. Dieses ruht aber auf einer tiefer-
en Schicht, welche nicht mehr persönlicher Erfahrung und
Erwerbung enstammt, sondern angeboren ist Diese tiefere
Schicht ist das sogenannte kollektive Unbewußte.*
A certain superficial level of the unconscience is
without doubt personal. I call it the personal

unconscious. But this personal unconscious rests upon a deeper level, which does not derive from personal experience and is not a personal acquisition but is inborn. This deeper level I call the collective unconscious.

Franz Kafka (1883-1924)

Alle streben doch nach dem Gesetz.
Everyone strives for the law.
　Der Prozeß

Als Gregor Samsa eines Morgens aus unruhigen Traümen erwachte, fand er sich in seinem Bett zu einem ungeheuren Ungeziefer verwandelt.
When Gregor Samsa woke one morning from restless dreams, he found himself transformed in his bed into a gigantic insect.
　Die Verwandlung

Es is oft besser, in Ketten als frei zu sein.
It is often better to be in chains than to be free.
　Der Prozeß

Jemand mußte Josef K. verleumdet haben, denn ohne daß er etwas Boses getan hätte, wurde er eines Morgens verhaftet.
Someone must have slandered Joseph K., for without having done anything bad, he was arrested one morning.
　Ibid.

*Sie konnen einwenden, daß es ja überhaupt kein Verfahren
ist. Sie haben sehr recht, denn es ist ja nur ein Verfahren,
wenn ich es als solches anerkenne.*
You may object that this is really not a trial. You are
right. It is only a trial when I recognise it as such.
  Ibid.

*Wie ein Kind am Tischtuch zerrt, aber nichts gewinnt,
sondern nur die ganze Pracht hinunterwirft und sie sich für
immer unerreichbar macht.*
Like a child who tugs at the tablecloth but gains
nothing, only throwing its entire splendour to the
ground, thus making it permanently unattainable.
  Das Schloß

Immanuel Kant (1724-1804)
*Aus so krummem Holze, als woraus der Mensch gemacht
ist, kann nichts ganz Gerades gezimmert werden.*
From the crooked timber of humanity nothing straight
can ever be made.
  *Idee zu einer allgemeinen Geschichte in weltbürgerlicher
  Absicht*

*Endlich giebt es einen Imperativ, der, ohne irgend eine
andere durch ein gewisses Verhalten zu erreichende Absicht
als Bedingung zum Grunde zu legen, dieses Verhalten
unmittelbar begeitet, Dieser Imperativ ist categorisch...
Dieser Imperativ mag der Sittlichkeit heißen.*
Finally, there is an imperative which requires a certain
conduct immediately, without having as its condition

any other purpose to be attained by it. This imperative is categorical... This imperative may be called that of Morality.

Grundlegung zur Metaphysik der Sitten

Handle so, daß du die Menschheit, so wohl in deiner Person, als in der Person eines jeden andern, jederzeit zugleich als Zweck, niemals bloß als Mittel brauchest.
So act as to treat humanity, whether in thine own person or in that of another, always as an end, never as a means only.

Ibid.

Ich sol niemals anders verfahren, als so, daß ich auch wollen könne, meine Maxim solle ein allgemeines Gesetz werden.
I must act only according to those principles which I could wish universal.

Ibid.

Wer den Zweck will, will (so fern die Vernunft auf seine Handlungen enschei-denden Einfluß hat), auch das dazu unent-behrlich nothwendige Mittel, das in seiner Gewalt ist.
Whoever wills the end, wills also (so far as reason decides his conduct) the means in his power which are indispensably necessary thereto.

Ibid.

Zwein Dinge erfüllen das Gemüt mit immer neuer und
zunehmender
Bewunderung und Ehrfurcht, je öfter und anhaltender sich

*das Nachdenken damit beschäftigt: der bestirnte Himmel
über mir, und das moralische Gesetz in mir.*
Two things fill the mind with ever new and increasing
wonder and awe, the more often and the more
seriously reflection concentrates upon them: the starry
heaven above me and the moral law within me.
   Kritik der praktischen Vernunft

Erich Kästner (1899-1974)
*Arbeit ist das halbe Leben,
Und die andre Hälfte auch.*
Work is half of life – and the other half, too.
   Burger, schont eure Anlagen

*Wenn Frauen Fehler machen wollen,
Dann soll man ihnen nicht in Wegw stehen.*
If women want to make mistakes, one should not
stand in their way.
   *Bei Durchsicht meiner Bücher 'Hotelsolo für eine
   Männerstimme*

Christoph Kaufmann (1753-95)
Sturm und Drang.
Storm and stress.

Julius Kell
Die Gründe kenne ich nicht, aber ich muß sie mißbilligen.
I do not know the reasons, but I have to disapprove of
them.
   February 1849, to the state parliament of Saxony

John F Kennedy (1917-63)
Ich bin ein Berliner.
I am a citizen of Berlin. (But 'Berliner' also means a kind of doughnut.)
   26 June 1963, in Berlin

Justinus Kerner (1786-1862)
Ade, nun, Ihr Lieben! Geschieden muß sein.
So goodbye, my loved ones! We must part.
   Wanderlied

Gottfried Kinkel (1815-82)
Sein Schicksal schafft sich selbst der Mann.
Man creates his own destiny.
   Otto der Schütz

Heinrich von Kleist (1777-1811)
Ist dir ein Heiligtum ganz unbekannt,
Das, in dem Lager, Vaterland sich nennt?
Is that holy place quite unknown to you which, within our camp, is called Fatherland?
   Prinz Friedrich von Homburg

Arthur Koestler (1905-83)
Gäbe es das Wort 'Tod' in unserem Sprachschatz nicht wären die großen Werke der Literatur nie geschrieben worden.
If the word 'death' did not exist in our vocabulary, the great works of literature would never have been written.
   Mensch

Erwin Guido Kolbenheyer (1878-1962)

Die gleiche weiße Decke aller Straßen,
Hüllt und bedeckt die Mühsal auf der Erde.
Es stirbt ein Jahr, lautlos, entsühnt, gelassen,
Gibt dem Geschicke heim, was dauert werde.

The same white blanket on all the streets shrouds and covers earthly tribulations. A year is dying, silently, expiated and calm, returning to fate that which will endure.

   Wintersonnenwende

Karl Kraus (1874-1936)

Mir fällt zu Hitler nichts ein... Ich fühle mich wie vor den Kopf geschlagen.

I can't think of anything to say about Hitler... I feel as though I have been hit over the head.

   Die Fackel, July 1934

Gotthold Ephraim Lessing (1729-81)

Der wahre Bettler ist
Doch einzig und allein der wahre König!

The true beggar is the only true king.

   Nathan der Weise

Es ist nicht wahr, daß die kürzeste Linie immer die gerade ist.

It is not true that the shortest line is always the straightest.

   Die Erziehung des Menschengeschlechts

Jeder liebt sich selber nur am meisten.

Everyone loves himself the most.

   Nathan der Weise

Robert Ley (1890-1945)
Kraft durch Freude.
Strength through joy.
  German Labour Front slogan from 1933

Georg Christoph Lichtenberg (1742-99)
Acht Bände hat er geschrieben. Er hätte gewiß besser getan,
er hätte acht Bäume gepflanzt oder acht Kinder erzeugt.
He has written eight volumes. He would surely have
done better to plant eight trees, or produce eight
children.
  Aphorismen (of himself)

Das älteste Sprichwort ist wohl: Allzuviel ist ungesund.
The old proverb is right: excess is unhealthy.
  Ibid.

Das Buch ist ein Spiegel; wenn ein Affe hineinguckt, so
kann freilich kein Apostel heraussehen.
A book is a mirror; if an ape looks into it, an apostle
cannot look out of it.
  Ibid.

Das Sorgenschränkchen, das Allerheiligste der innersten
Seelenökonomie, das nur des Nachts geöffnet wird.
The little cupboard of worries, the inner sanctum of
the soul's innermost economy, which is opened only
at night.
  Ibid.

Der Glaube an einen Gott ist Instinkt, er ist dem Menschen
natürlich, so wie das Gehen auf zwei Beinen.
Belief in a god is instinctive; it is as natural to
mankind as walking on two legs.

    Ibid.

Der Weisheit erster Schritt ist: alles anzuklagen.
Der letzte ist: sich mit allem zu vertragen.
The first step of wisdom is to accuse everything. The
last is to come to terms with everything.

    Ibid.

Die barbarische Genauigkeit; winselnde Demut.
Barbaric precision; whimpering humility!

    Ibid.

Die Gelehrsamkeit kann auch ins Laub treiben, ohne Früchte
zu tragen.
Erudition can also sprout leaves without bearing fruit.

    Ibid.

Die Wahrheit finden wollen ist Verdienst, wenn man auch
auf dem Wege irrt.
There is merit in wanting to discover the truth, even if
one makes mistakes along the way.

    Ibid.

Ein Grab ist doch immer die beste
Befestigung wider Stürme des Schicksals.
The grave, however, remains the best fortress against
the storms of fate.

    Ibid.

Eine seltsamere Ware als Bücher gibt es wohl schwerlich in der Welt. Von Leuten gedruckt, die sie nicht verstehen; von Leuten verkauft, die sie nicht verstehen; gebunden, rezensiert und gelesen von Leuten, die sie nicht verstehen; und nun gar geschrieben von Leuten, die sie nicht verstehen.

It would be difficult to find any products in the world that are as strange as books. Printed by people who don't understand them; sold by people who don't understand them; bound, reviewed and read by people who don't understand them; and now, even written by people who don't understand them.

Ibid.

Einen Menschen recht zu verstehen, müßte man zuweilen der nämliche Mensch sein, den man verstehen will.

To understand a man properly, one would need sometimes to be the person one wants to understand.

Ibid.

Gott schafft die Tiere, der Mensch schafft sich selber.

God creates the animals, man creates himself.

Ibid.

Gott schuf den Menschen nach seinem Bilde, das heißt vermutlich, der mensch schuf Gott nach dem seinigen.

God created man in his own image; this presumably means that man created God in his own image.

Ibid.

Heftige Ehrgeiz und Mißtrauen habe ich noch allemal beisammen gesehen.

I have always seen burning ambition accompanies by distrust.

   Ibid.

Ich glaube, daß die Quelle des meisten menschlichen Elends in Indolenz und Weichlichkeit liegt. Die Nation, die die meiste Spannkraft hatte, war auch allezeit die freiste und glcklicste.

I believe that the source of most human misery lies in indolence and weakness. The nation that had the most vigour was always the freest and the happiest too.

   Ibid.

Ich kenne die Leute wohl, die ihr meint; sie sind bloß Geist und Theörie und können sich keinen Knopf annähen.

I know the people well whom you mean: they are just intellect and theory and could not sew on a button for themselves.

   Ibid.

Jeder Mensch hat auch seine moralische 'Backside', die er nicht ohne Not zeigt, und die er solange als möglich mit der Hosen des guten Anstandes zudeckt.

Every person also has his moral 'backside', which he does not expose needlessly, and which he covers for as long as possible with the trousers of politeness.

   Ibid.

Nicht bloß wissen, sondern auch für die Nachwelt tun, was die Vorwelt für uns getan hat, heißt ein Mensch sein.
Being a man means not just knowing, but also doing for posterity, that which our predecessors did for us.
Ibid.

Ordnung führt zu allen Tugenden! Aber was führt zur Ordnung?
Order leads to all virtues. But what leads to order?
Ibid.

Viele Unternehmungen mißlingen bloß, weil man die Früchte davon noch gerne erleben wollte.
Many enterprises fail simply through eagerness to experience their fruits.
Ibid.

Wo Mäßigung ein Fehler ist, da ist Gleichgültigkeit ein Verbrechen.
If restraint is weakness, indifference is a crime.
Ibid.

Wohin wir nur sehen, so sehen wir bloß uns.
Wherever we look, we can only see ourselves.
Ibid.

Friedrich von Logau
Gottes Mühlen mahlen langsam, mahlen aber trefflich klein.
The mills of God grind slowly, yet they grind exceeding small.

In Gefahr und großer Not bringt der Mittelweg Tod.
In times of danger and great distress, compromise will
bring death.

Konrad Lorenz (1903-89)
Überhaupt ist es für den Froscher ein guter Morgensport,
täglichvor dem Frühstück eine Lieblingshypothese einzu-
stampfen – daserhält jung.
It is generally a good morning exercise for a scientist
to discard some pet theory every day before breakfast-
it keeps him young.

Martin Luther (1483-1546)
Die Kunst geht nach Brod.
Art comes after bread.

Ein feste Burg ist unser Gott.
A strong citadel is our God.

Hier stehe ich, ich kann nicht anders. Gott helfe mir. Amen
Here I stand – I can do nought else. God help me.
Amen.
  1521 in Worms

Mönchlein, Mönchlein, du gehst einen schweren Gang.
Little monk, little monk, you are following a difficult
path.
  On the eve of his departure for Worms

Wo steht das geschrieben?
Where is it written?
  Kleinen Katechismus and Lehrstück von Amt der Schlüssel

73

Rosa Luxemburg (1870-1919)
Freiheit ist immer nur Freiheit des anders Denkenden.
Freedom is always and only the freedom to think differently.

Thomas Mann (1875-1955)
Komme, Tod, und raub mich, Tod, im Kuße!
Come, death, carry me off in your kiss!
   Der Kamerad

Karl Marx (1818-83)
Die Geschichte aller bisherigen Gesellschaft ist die Geschichte von Klassenkämpfen.
The history of all previous society is the history of class war.
   Manifest der Kommunistischen Partei (with Friedrich Engels)

Die Philosophen haben die Welt nur verschieden interpretiert; es kommt aber darauf an, sie zu verändern.
The philosophers have merely interpreted the world in different ways. Changing it is what matters, however.
   Thesen über Feuerbach

Die Proletarier haben nichts zu verlieren als ihre Ketten.
The proletariat have nothing to lose except their chains.
   Manifest der Kommunistischen Partei (with Friedrich Engels)

Die Religion...ist das Opium des Volkes.
Religion...is the opium of the people.
   Zur Kritik der Hegelschen Rechtsphilosophie Einleitung

Ein Gespenst geht um in Europa – das Gespenst des Kommunismus.
A spectre is haunting Europe – the spectre of communism.
   Manifest der Kommunistischen Partei (with Friedrich Engels)

Es ist nicht das Bewußtsein der Menschen, das ihr Sein, sondern umgekehrt ihr gesellschaftliches Sein, das ihr Bewußtsein bestimmt.
It is not the consciousness of men that determines their existence; it is the other way round: their collective existence determines their consciousness.
   Vorwort: Zur Kritik der politischen Ökonomie

Wilhelm von Merckel (1803-61)
Gegen Demokraten helfen nur Soldaten.
Soldiers are the only protection against democrats.
   Die fünfte Zunft

Prince Metternich (1773-1859)
Der Kaiser ist Alles, Wien ist nichts!
The Emperor is everything, Vienna is nothing!

Deutschland, ein geographischer Begriff.
Germany is a geographical expression.
   About the country's disunity; he said the same about Italy

Agnes Miegel (1879-1964)
Gott heilt dein und mein Leben
Wie Blumen in seiner Hand.
God held my life and your life like flowers in his hand.
   Blumen

Johann Martin Miller (1750-1814)

Je mehr er hat, je mehr er will,
Nie schweigen seine Klagen still.
The more he has the more he wants; his complaints never cease.

Zufriedenheit

Helmuth von Moltke (1848-1916)

Der ewige Friede ist ein Traum und nicht einmal ein schöner.
Eternal peace is a dream, and not even a nice one.

Letter to Johann Kaspar Bluntschli, 11 December 1880

Erst Wägen und dann wagen.
Look before you leap. (Lit. First weigh it up, then act)

Maxim

Wolfgang Amadeus Mozart (1756-91)

Hütet Euch vor Weibertücken!
Beware women's waywardness.

Libretto of Die Zauberflöte

Friedrich Nietzsche (1844-1900)

Also sprach Zarathustra.
Thus spoke Zarathustra.

Also sprach Zarathustra

Auf dem Grunde aller dieser vornehmen
Rassen ist das Raubtier, die prachtvolle nach Beute und
Sieg lüstern schweifende blonde Bestie nich zu verkennen.
At the base of all these aristocratic races the predator is not to be mistaken, the splendrous blond beast,

avidly rampant for plunder and victory.

Zur Genealogie der Moral

*Aus der Kriegsschule des Lebens – was mich nicht
umbringt, macht mich stärker.*
From the war-school of life – whatever does not kill
me makes me stronger.

*Götzen-Dämmerung oder Wie man mit dem Hammer
philosophiert*

Das Weib war der zweite Fehlgriff Gottes.
Woman was God's second blunder.

Der Antichrist

*Ich lehre euch den Ubermenschen. Der Mensch ist etwas,
das überwunden werden soil.*
I teach you the superman. Man is something that has
to be overcome.

Also sprach Zarathustra

*Die Krähen schrein
Und Ziehen schwirren Flugs zur Stadt:
Bald wird es schnein.
Wohl dem, der jetzt noch Heimat hat!*
The crows shriek and move towards the town in
whirling flight. Soon it will snow. Happy is he who still
has a home.

Vereinsamt

Du gehst zu Frauen? Vergiß die Peitsche nicht!
You are going to a woman? Do not forget the whip!

Also Sprach Zarathustra

Glaubt es mir! – das Geheimnis, um die größte
Fruchtbarkeit und den größten Genuß vom Dasein
einzuernten, heißt: gefährlich leben!
Believe me! The secret if reaping the most fruitful
harvest and the greatest enjoyment from life is to live
dangerously.

   Die fröhliche Wissenschaft

Gott ist tot! Und wir haben ihn getötet!
God is dead! God will remain dead! And we have
killed him!

   Ibid.

Herren-Moral and Sklaven-Moral.
Master-morality and slave-morality.

   Jenseits von Gut und Böse

Im echten Manne ist ein Kind versteckt: das will spielen.
Auf, ihr Frauen, so entdeckt mir doch das Kind im Manne!
A child is hidden in the real man, and it wants to play.
Come on, you women, discover the child in the man!

   Also sprach Zarathustra

Wer sich stets viel geschont hat, der kränkelt zuletzt an
seiner vielen Schonung. Gelobt sei, was hart macht.
He who has always cushioned himself will in the end
become sick of his great indulgence. That which
makes things hard should be praised.

   Ibid.

Novalis (Friedrich von Hardenberg) (1772-1801)

Mensch werden ist eine Kunst.

Becoming a human is an art.

Fragmente

Nach innen geht der geheimnisvolle Weg. In uns oder nirgends ist die Ewigkeit mit ihren Welten, die Vergangenheit und Zukunft.

The secret path leads inwards. In us and nowhere else lies eternity, with its past and future worlds.

Heinrich von Ofterdingen

Oft fühl ich jetzt... [und] je tiefer ich einsehe, daß Schicksal und Gemüt Namen eines Begriffes sind.

I often feel, and ever more deeply I realize, that fate and character are the same conception.

Ibid.

Wenige wissen
Das Geheimnis der Liebe,
Fühlen Unersättlichkeit
Und ewigen Durst.

Few know the secret of love; they feel insatiability and perpetual thirst.

Hymme

Ernst Penzoldt (1892-1955)

In Erstaunen setzen, ist das nicht die Natur des Poeten?

Is it not the nature of poets to astonish?

Der Delphin

Proverbs

Alle Macht kommt vom Volke.
All power comes from the people.

Allen zu glauben ist zu viel, keinem glauben zu wenig.
To believe everyone is too much, believing no one is
too little.

Alles oder nichts!
All or nothing!
   Expression

Arbeit macht frei.
Work liberates.
   Inscription over the gates of Dachau (and subsequently
   those of Auschwitz), 1933

Das allgemeine Verhältnis erkennet nur Gott.
Only God understands the overall relationship of things.

Das freie Meer befreit den Geist.
The free ocean releases the spirit.

Das Ganze macht, nicht das Einzelne.
It is the whole, not the detail, which counts.

Denken ist danken.
To think is to thank.

Der Mensch denkt, Gott lenkt.
Man proposes, God disposes. (Lit. Man thinks, God
directs.)

Ein Fuchs riecht den andern.
One fox smells another.

Ersatz für's Unersätzliche.
A replacement for the irreplaceable.

Erst wenn du dich selbst erkannt, Verurteile deinen Nächsten.
Only when you have understood yourself can you
judge your neighbour.

Es ist nicht leicht, mensch zu sein.
Being human is not easy.

Guten Kaufs macht den Beutel leer.
Good purchases make empty purses.

Heut dies und morgen das.
Today this and tomorrow that.

Im Kleinen liegt das Große.
Greatness lies in small things.

In der Natur ist alles einzeln.
In nature everything is individual.

Jeder ist Kaiser in seiner Lage.
Everyone is king in his own camp.

*Jeder Mensch glaubt, weil er spricht, über die Sprache
sprechen zu dürfen.*
Everyone believes that because he can speak, he may
talk about language.

Kleiner mann hat auch sein Stolz.
The little man also has his pride.

Lieber ein kleiner Herr als ein großer Knecht.
It is better to be a minor lord than an important
servant.

Pack schlägt sich, Pack verträgt sich.
The rabble is at each other's throats one minute, and
friends again the next.

Was man aufgibt, hat man nie verloren.
What one sacrifices is never lost.

Wehret den Anfängen.
Beware of beginnings.

Weisheit kommt nicht gratis mit dem Alter
Wisdom does not come free with age.

Zeit ist teuer.
Time is expensive.

Zufriedenheit geht über Reichtum.
Contentment is worth more than riches.

Wilhelm Raabe (1831-1910)
*Das Schicksal benutzt meistens doch unsere schwachen Punkte,
um uns auf das uns Dienliche aufmerksam zu machen.*
Fate generally uses our weak points to teach us
something useful.
  Stopfkuchen

Sieh nach den Sternen! Gib acht auf die Gassen!
Look to the stars! Keep an eye on the alleyways!
Die Leute aus dem Walde

Waiter Rathenau (1867-1922)
An diesem Tage hatte die Weltgeschichte ihren Sinn verloren.
On this day the history of the world seems to have lost
its mind.
On the outbreak of the First World War

Jean Paul Richter (1763-1825)
*Wer den kleinsten Theil eines Geheimnisses hingibt, hat den
andern nicht mehr in der Gewalt.*
When one reveals the smallest part of a secret one can
no longer be said to possess the rest of it.

Rainer Maria Rilke (1875-1926)
*Alles
Ist nicht es selbst.*
Everything is not itself.
Duineser Elegien

Alles Erworbene bedroht die Maschine.
Machines threaten everything that has ever been
achieved.
Die Sonette an Orpheus

*Das strebende Stemmen,
Grau aus vergehender Stadt oder aus fremder, des Doms.*
The striving grey mass of the cathedral rising from a
strange or dying town.
Duineser Elegien

Die großen Worte aus den Zeiten, da Geschehen noch
sichtbar war, sind nicht für uns. Wer spricht von Siegen?
Überstehn ist alles.
Those great words from the times when we could see
what was going to happen are not for us. Who speaks
of victories? Survival is everything.
  Requiem für Wolf, Graf von Kalckreuth

Du mußt dein Leben ändern!
You must change your life!
  Archaischer Torso Apollos

Einsam steigt er dahin, in die Berge des Urleids,
Und nicht einmal sein Schritt klingt aus dem tonlosen Los.
Lonely he climbs the mountains of primeval sorrow,
and not even his footsteps ring out from the
tonelessness of destiny.
  Duineser Elegien

Ein jeder Engel ist schrecklich.
Every angel is frightening.
  Ibid.

Herr: Es ist Zeit. Der Sommer war sehr groß.
Leg deinen Schatten auf die Sonnenuhren,
Und auf den Fluren laß die Winde los.
Lord, it is time! It was a great summer. Lay your
shadows across the sundials, and unleash the winds
across the open fields.
  Herbsttag

So leben wir und nehmen immer Abschied.
So we live, forever saying goodbye.
   Duineser Elegien

Wer saß nicht bang vor seines Herzens Vorhang?
Who has not sat in uneasy anticipation before the
stage curtain of his heart?
   Ibid.

Wunderlich nah ist der Held doch den jugendlich Toten.
The hero is strangely close to those who died young.
   Ibid.

Friedrich Rückert (1788-1866)
Dem Wandersmann gehört die Welt
In allen ihren Weiten.
To the wanderer belongs the whole wide world.

Albrecht Schaeffer (1885-1930)
Tiefe Nacht ist drauß und drinnen,
Tiefe Nacht in euren Sinnen,
Tiefe Nacht allumgetan.
Deep night is outside and inside, deep night is in your
consciousness, deep night is complete.
   Die lange Nacht

Friedrich von Schelling (1775-1854)
Architektur ist überhaupt die erstarrte Musik.
Architecture is frozen music.

Ferdinand von Schill (1776-1809)
Lieber ein Ende mit Schrecken als ein Schrecken ohne Ende.
Better a terrifying end than terror without end.
   To his troops in 1809

Freidrich Schiller (1759-1805)
Ach, es geschehen keine Wunder mehr!
Alas, miracles no longer happen!
   Die Jungfrau von Orleans

Alle Menschen werden Brüder.
All men will become brothers.
   An die Freude

Anklagen ist mein Amt und meine Sendung.
Accusation is my duty and my mission.
   Wallenstein

Auch das Schöne muß sterben!
Even beauty must die!
   Nänie

Beim wunderbaren Gott! Das Weib ist schön.
By the wonderful God! Women are beautiful.

Bettler sind Könige.
Beggars are kings.
   Die Räuber

Da rast der See und will sein Opfer haben.
The sea is raging and demands its sacrifice.
   Wilhelm Tell

Das alte stürzt, es ändert sich die Zeit.
The old order is crumbling; times are changing.
  Ibid.

*Das Gesetz hat noch keinen großen Mann gebildet, aber
die Freiheit brütet Kolosse und Extremitäten aus.*
Laws have never yet produced a great man, but
freedom incubates both giants and extremists.
  Die Räuber

Dem Herzen folg'ich, denn ich darf ihm trauen.
I follow my heart, for I can trust it.
  Wallensteins Tod

Denn nur vom Nutzen wird die Welt regiert.
The world is ruled only according to profit.
  Ibid.

Der brave Mann denkt an sich selbst zuletzt.
The good man thinks of himself last.
  Wilhelm Tell

*Der Mensch spielt nur, woe r in voller Bedeutung des Worts
Mensch ist, und er ist nur da ganz Mensch, wo er spielt.*
Man plays only where he is, in the full sense of the word,
human, and he is an entire man only there where he plays.
  *Über die ästhetische Erziehung des Menschen in einer Reihe
  von Briefen*

Der Soldat allein ist der freie Mann.
The soldier is the only free man.
  Wallensteins Lager

Der Wahn ist kurz, die Reu ist lang.
The illusion [of love] is brief, the repentance long.

Die Geschichte der Welt ist sich selbst gleich wie die Gesetze
der Natur und einfach wie die Seele des Menschen.
Dieselben
The history of the world itself resembles the laws of
nature and is simple, like the human soul. The same
conditions bring back the same phenomena.
  Bedingungen bringen dieselben Erscheinungen zurück.
  Lecture, 1789

Die Gesetze der Welt sind Würfelspiele worden.
The laws of the world have become games of dice.
  Die Räuber

Die Natur gab die Schönheit des Baues,
die Seele gibt die Schönheit des Spiels.
Nature gave constructive work its beauty; the soul
gives beauty to playfulness.
  Über Anmut und Würde

Die schöne Seele hat kein anderes Verdienst, als daß sie ist.
A beautiful soul has no other merit than its existence.
  Ibid.

Die Schönheit gibt schlechterdings kein einzelnes Resultat
weder für den Verstand noch für den Willen, sie führt
keinen einzelnen, weder intellektuellen noch moralischen
Zweck aus, sie findet keine einzige Wahrheit, hilft uns keine
einzige Pflicht erfüllen und ist, mit einem Worte, gleich

ungeschickt, den Charakter zu gründen und den Kopf
aufzuklären.
Beauty has absolutely no result, either for the intellect
or for the will; it pursues no purpose, neither
intellectual nor moral; it uncovers no truth, does not
help us fulfil any duty and is, in a word, unsuited to
form the character or to enlighten the mind.
  Werke

Die sieht den Menschen in des Lebens Drang
Und wälzt die größre Hälfte seiner Schuld
Den unglückseligen Gestirnen zu.
Art sees men amid life's struggle, and shifts the greater
part of their guilt on to the hapless stars.
  Wallenstein

Die Treue, sie ist doch kein leere Wahn.
Loyalty is, however, no empty illusion.
  Die Bürgschaft

Die Weltgeschichte ist das Weltgericht
The history of the world is the judgement seat of the
world.
  Resignation

Dort erblick' ich schöne Hügel
Ewig jung und ewig grün!
Hätt' ich schwingen, hätt ich Flügel,
Nach den Hügeln zög' ich hin!
I saw there beautiful hills that were eternally young
and eternally green. If I had wings I would fly to them.
  Sehnsucht

Ein Diadem erkämpfen ist groß. Es wegwerfen ist göttlich.
To win a crown is greatness. To throw it away is
godlike.
   Fiesko

Ein freies Leben ist ein paar knechtischer Stunden wert.
A life of freedom is worth a few hours of servitude.
   Fiesko

Ein jeder wird besteuert nach Vermögen.
Everyone will be taxed according to his means.
   Wilhelm Tell

Ein rechter hilft sich selbst.
A true marksman helps himself.
   Ibid.

Eine notwendige Operation des Dichters ist Idealisierung
seines Gegenstandes, ohne welche er aufhört seinen Namen
zu verdienen.
A necessary process of what poets do is to idealise
their subject – without which they no longer deserve
the name.
   Review of GA Bürger's Gedichte

Englands Beherrscher brauchen nichts zu scheuen, als ihr
Gewissen und ihr Parlament.
England's rulers need fear nothing except their
conscience and their parliament.
   Maria Stuart

Er ging auf wie ein Meteor und schwindet wie eine sinkende Sonne.

He rose like a meteor and faded away like the setting sun.

Review of a production of Die Räuber

Erloschen sind die heitern Sonnen,
Die meiner Jugend Pfad erhellt.

The cheerful sunshine that brightened my young path has been extinguished.

Die Ideale

Freude heißt die starker Feder
In der ewigen Natur,
Freude, Freude, treibt die Räder
In der großen Weltenuhr.

Joy is the powerful spring of eternal nature; joy, joy drives the wheels of the great world clock.

An die Freude

Gefährlich ist's, den Leu zu wecken,
Verderblich ist des Tigers Zahn,
Jedoch der schrecklichste der Schrecken,
Das ist der Mensch in Seinem Wahn.

It is dangerous to awaken a lion, and the tiger's tooth is sharp, but the most terrible of all terrors is the mania of man.

Das Lied von der Glocke

Gehorsam ist des Christen Schmuck.

Obedience is the ornament of the Christian.

Der Kampf mit dem Drachen

Groß kann man sich im Glück, erhaben nur im Unglück zeigen.
One can show oneself to be great in times of good fortune, but merely noble in times of misfortune.
   Vom Erhabenen

Ich aber soll zum Meißel mich erniedern,
Wo ich der Künstler könnte sein?
Why should I lower myself to the level of a chisel, when I could be the artist?
   Werke

Ich bin mein Himmel und meine Hölle.
I am my heaven and my hell.
   Die Räuber

Ja süß, himmlisch süß ists, eingewiegt zu werden in den Schlaf des Todes von dem Gesang des Geliebten.
Yes, it is sweet, heavenly sweet, to be rocked into the sleep of death by the songs of one's beloved.
   Ibid.

Jeder Affekt hat seine spezifiken Äußerungen und, so zu sagen, seinen eigentümlichen Dialekt, an dem man ihn kennt.
Every emotion has its specific expression and, so to speak, its characteristic dialect, by which one recognises it.
   Werke

*Jetzt ergeht es ihm wie jedem Schwärmer, der von seiner
herrschenden Idee überwältigt wird. Er kennt keine
Grenzen mehr.*
Now he is becoming like every zealot who is over-
whelmed by his ruling idea. He no longer recognises
any limits.

   Ibid.

Man löst sich nicht allmählich von dem Leben!
One cannot gradually release oneself from life.

   Ibid.

Mein Geist dürstet nach Taten, mein Atem nach Freiheit.
My spirit yearns for action, my breath for freedom.

   Die Räuber

*Mein Handwerk ist Wiedervergeltung – Rache ist mein
Gewerbe.*
My trade is retaliation; revenge is my profession.

   Ibid.

Mit der Dummheit kämpfen Götter selbst vergebens.
Against stupidity even the gods struggle in vain.

   Die Jungfrau von Orleans

*Mit gewaltsamer Hand
Löset der Mord auch das heiligste Band.*
Murder dissolves even the most sacred bond with its
violent hands.

   Die Braut von Messina

Naiv muß jedes wahre Genie sein.
Every true genius must be naïve
  Über naïve und sentimentalische Dichtung

O über mich Narren, de rich wähnete, die Welt duch
Greuel zu verschönen und die Gesetze durch Gesetzlosigkeit
aufrecht zu halten. Ich nannte es Rache und Recht.
Oh how foolish I was to dream that I could make the
world more beautiful by means of atrocity and that I
could uphold the law by means of lawlessness. I called
it revenge and justice.
  Die Räuber

Reue und Verzweiflung über ein begangenes Verbrechen
zeigen uns die Macht des Sittengesetzes nur später, nicht
schwächer.
Remorse and despair about having committed a crime
reveal the power of the moral law belatedly, but no
less forcefully.
  Werke

So geschieht es denn nicht selten, das [der Idealist] über
dem unbegrenzten Ideale den begrenzten Fall der
Anwendung über-siehet und, von einem Maximum erfüllt,
das Minimum verabsäumt, aus dem noch alles Große in
der Wirklichkeit erwächst.
It often happens that [the idealist], filled with limitless
idealism, overlooks the practical limits of application,
and, inspired by the maximum, neglects the
minimum, from which, after all, grows everything that
is great in the real world.
  Über naïve und sentimentalische Dichtung

So ist jede schöne Gabe
Flüchtig wie des Blitzes Schein,
Schnell in ihrem düstern Grabe
Schließt die Nacht sie wieder ein.
Thus every beautiful talent is as fleeting as a flash of
lightning, and is quickly enclosed again in night's
gloomy grave.

   Die Gunst des Augenblicks

So kann es Leute geben, die zuletzt mechanisch
Gutes oder Böses tun.
Therefore there are people who, in the end, do good
or evil quite mechanically.

   Werke

Sphären in einander lenkt die Liebe,
Weltsysteme dauern nur durch sie.
Love guides the spheres together, and world systems
endure only through love.

   Phantasie an Laura

Sprich mir von allen Schrecken des Gewissens, von meinem
Vater sprich mir nicht.
Tell me about all the terrors of the conscious mind,
but do not speak of my father.

   Don Karlos

Todes angst ist ärger als Sterben.
The fear of death is worse than dying.

   Die Räuber

Überhaupt beobachtet man, daß die
Bösartigkeit der Seele gar oft in kranken Körpern wohnt.
One can generally observe that maliciousness of the
soul often dwells in sick bodies.

Verstücke den Donner in seine einfache Silben, und du
wirst Kinder damit in der Schlummer singen; schmelze sie
zusammen in einen plötzlichen Schall, und der
monarchische Laut wird den ewigen Himmel bewegen.
Divide the thunder into its simple syllables, and you
will be able to sing children to sleep with them; but,
melt them together into one sudden roar, and the
royal sound will move the eternal heavens.
    Fiesko

Was den politischen Enthusiasten bewegt, ist nicht was er
siehet, sondern was er denkt.
What moves the political enthusiast is not what he
sees, but what he thinks.
    Werke

Was Hände bauten, können Hände stürzen.
What hands have built, hands can cause to fall.
    Wilhelm Tell

Was man scheint, hat jedermann zum Richter, was man ist,
hat keinen.
Everyone judges you by how you appear, no one
judges by what you are.
    Maria Stuart

Was unsterblich im Gesang soll leben,
Muß im Leben untergehn.
What is immortalised in song must be destroyed in life.
   Die Götter Griechenlands

Welch Haupt steht fort, wenn dieses heil'ge fiel?
Whose head will remain upright if this blessed one
were to fall?
   Maria Stuart

Wer gar zuviel bedenkt, wird wenig leisten.
He who reflects too much will achieve little.
   Wilhelm Tell

Willst du dich selber erkennen, so sieh, wie die Andern es
treiben; Willst du die Andern verstehn, blick'in dein eigenes
Herz.
If you want to know yourself, see how others behave;
if you want to understand others, look in your own
heart!

Alfred von Schlieffen (1833-1913)
Macht mir den rechten Flügel stark!
Make the right wing strong for me!
   1913, on his death bed

Max Schnekkenburger (1819-1849)
Lieb Vaterland, magst ruhig sein
Fest steht und treu die Wacht am Rhein.
Dear Fatherland, you can be calm, for the watch
stands firm and faithful on the Rhine.
   Die Wacht am Rhein

Louis Schnieder

O Tannenbaum, O Tannenbaum,
Wie grün sind deine Blätter!
O pinetree, o pinetree,
How green are thy leaves.

Der Kurmärker und die Picarde

Wolfdietrich Schnurre (1920-89)

Galgenhumor gibt es nicht. Wer ihn zu haben glaubt, hängt schon.
Gallows humour does not exist; whoever believes that he possesses it will soon hang.

Der Schattenfotograf

Artur Schopenhauer (1788-1860)

Alles was geschieht, vom Größten bis zum Kleinsten, geschieht nothwendig.
Everything that happens, from the greatest to the least, happens inevitably.

Die meisten Menschen sind so subjektiv, daß im Grunde nichts Interesse für sie hat, als ganz allein sie selbst.
Most men are so subjective that fundamentally nothing interests them except themselves.

Die unbegrenzte Welt, voll Leiden überall, in unendlicher Vergangenheit, in unendlicher Zukunft.
The limitless world, everywhere full of suffering, in an unending past, in an unending future.

Die Welt als Wille und Vorstellung

Höflichkeit ist Klugheit; folglich ist Unhöflichkeit Dummheit.
Politeness is wisdom, therefore impoliteness is folly.

*Jeder ist werth, daß man ihn aufmerksam betrachte; wenn
auch nicht Jeder, daß man mit ihm redet.*
Every man is worth careful study; but not every man
is worth talking to.

Albert Schweitzer (1875-1965)
*Am Abend des dritten Tages, als wir bei Sonnenuntergang
gerade durch eine Herde Nilpferde hindurchfuhren, stand
urplötzlich, von mir nicht geahnt und nicht gesucht, das
Wort 'Ehrfurcht vor dem Leben' vor mir.*
Late on the third day, at the very moment when, at
sunset, we were making our way through a herd of
hippopotami, there flashed upon my mind, unexpected
and unsought, the phrase, 'Reverence for Life'.
  Aus meinem Leben und Denken

FW von der Schulenburg-Kehnert (1742-1815)
*Der König hat eine Bataille verloren. Jetzt ist die Ruhe die
erste Bürgerpflicht.*
The king has lost a battle. Calm is now the primary
duty of all citizens.
  7 October 1806, after the battle of Jena and Auerstedt

Theodor Storm (1817-88)
Der eine fragt: Was kommt danach?
Der andere fragt nur: Ist es recht?
Und so unterscheidet sich
Der Freie von dem Knecht.

One person asks 'What happens next?' The other asks only, 'Is it right?' And the free man is thus distinguished from the serf.

Der eine fragt: Was kommt danach?

Halte fest: du hast vom Leben doch am Ende nur dich selber.
Hold fast: in the end all you will have from life is yourself.

Für meine Söhne

Liebe ist nichts als Angst des sterblichen Menschen vor dem Alleinsein.
Love is nothing but the human fear of being alone.

Im Schloß

Otto Strasser (1897-1974)
Er sagt, was das Herz seiner Zuhörer zu hören wünscht.
He says what the heart of his audience wants to hear.

Of Hitler, 1930

Gustav Stresemann (1878-1929)
Zum erstenmal einen Silberstreifen an dem sonst düsteren Horizont.
For the first time we can see a silver streak on the otherwise murky horizon.

1924, after the second London conference on war reparations

Kurt Tucholsky (1890-1935)
Die deutsche Revolution hat im Saale stattgefunden.
The German revolution took place in a room.

Schnipsel, 'Wir Negativen'

Johann Ludwig Uhland (1787-1862)
Als wär's ein Stück von mir.
As if it were part of me.
  Ich hatt' einen Kameraden

Ich hatt einen Kamaraden,
Einen bessern find'st du nicht.
Die Trommel schlug zum streite,
er ging an meiner Seite
In gleichem schritt und Tritt.
I had a comrade, a better one you'd never find. When the drum called us to war, he marched beside me step by step.

Fritz Usinger (1895-1982)
Es weiß vielleicht ein Gott, wohin wir ziehn
Wir wissen nicht das Ziel und nicht zurück
Perhaps a god knows where we are going. We do not know our goal, or the way back.
  Große Elegie

Wilhelm Heinrich Wackenroder (1773-98)
Die Kunst ist eine verführerische, verbotene Frucht.
Art is a seductive, forbidden fruit.
  'Ein Brief Joseph Berglingers' in Phantasien über die Kunst,
  für Freunde der Kunst

Richard Wagner (1813-83)
Das Wunderreich der Nacht.
The wonder-realm of Night.
  Tristan und Isolde

Du bist der Lenz, nach dem ich verlangte.
You are the spring for which I longed.
> *Die Walküre*

Heiajoho! Grane! Grüß deinen Herren! Siegfried! Siegfried!
Sieh'! Selig grüßt dich dein Weib!
Heiajoho! Grane! Greet your master! Siegfried!
Siegfried! See! Joyfully you wife greets you!
> *Die Walküre (Brünnhilde's last words as she rides her*
> *horse, Grane, into Siegfried's funeral pyre)*

Hier gilt's der Kunst.
Art reigns here.
> *Die Meistersinger von Nürnberg*

O Minnetrug! O Lieberzung! Der Welt holdaster Wahn!
O deception of love! O passion's force! Most beautiful
of the world's illusions!
> *Tristan und Isolde*

O sink hernieder
Nacht der Liebe,
Gibt vergessen
Daß ich lebe.
Oh descend here, night of love, and let me forget that I
am alive.
> *Ibid.*

Ruhe, ruhe, du Gott!
Rest, rest, thou God!
> *Götterdämerung (Brünnhilde to Wotan)*

So stürben wir um ungetrennt, ewig einig ohne End', ohn'
Erwachen, ohn' Erbange, namelos in Lieb' umfangen, ganz
uns selbst gegeben, der lieb nur zu leben!
So might we die together, eternally, one without end,
without awakening, without fearing, nameless in love's
embrace, giving ourselves wholly, to live only for love.
   Tristan und Isolde

Vereint sind Liebe und Lenz!
Spring and love are made one!
   Die Walküre

Robert Walser (1878-1956)
Könnten Sie nicht ein wenig vergessen, berühmt zu sein?
Couldn't you forget your fame just a little?
   To Hugo von Hofmannsthal

Christoph Martin Wieland (1733-1813)
Ein einz'ger Augenblick kann alles umgestalten.
Everything can change in the blink of an eye.
   Oberon

Ludwig Wittgenstein (1889-1951)
Alles, was überhaupt gedacht werden kann, kann klar
gedacht werden.
Everything that can be thought at all can be thought
clearly.
   Tractatus logico-philosophicus

Das Bild ist ein Modell der Wirklichkeit.
A picture is a model of reality.
   Ibid.

*Der ganzen modernen Weltanschauung liegt die
Täuschungzugrunde, daß die sogennanten Naturgesetze die
Erklärungen der Naturerscheinungen seien.*
The entire modern world view supports an illusion
that the so-called laws of nature are the explanation of
natural phenomena.
   Ibid.

Der Gedanke ist der sinnvolle Satz.
A thought is a meaningful proposition.
   Ibid.

*Der Tod ist kein Ereignis des Lebens. Den Tod erlebt man
nicht.*
Death is not an event of life; one does not experience
death.
   Ibid.

Die gesamte Wirklichkeit ist die Welt.
The sum of reality is the world.
   Ibid.

Die Gesamtheit der wahren Gedanken istein Bild der Welt.
The totality of true thought is a picture of the world.
   Ibid.

*Die Grenzen meiner Sprache bedeuten die Grenzen meiner
Welt.*
The limits of my language mean the limits of my
world.
   Ibid.

Die Logik erfüllt die Welt; die Grenzen der Welt sind auch ihre Grenzen.
Logic fills the world; the limits of the world are its limits too.
   Ibid.

Die Philosophie ist ein Kampf gegen die Verhexung unseres Verstandes durch die Mittel unserer Sprache.
Philosophy is a battle against the bewitchment of our intelligence by means of language.
   Philosophische Untersuchungen

Die Philosophie ist keine Lehre, sondern eine Tätigkeit.
Philosophy is not a doctrine, but an occupation.
   Tractatus logico-philosophicus

Die Welt des Glücklichen ist eine andere als die des Unglüklichen.
The world of fortunate people is different from that of the unfortunate.
   Ibid.

Die Welt ist die Gesamtheit der Tatsachen, nicht der Dinge.
The world is the totality of facts, not of things.
   Ibid.

Die Welt ist unabhängig von meinem Willen
The world is independent of my will.
   Ibid.

Ethik und Ästhetik sind Eins.
Ethics and aesthetics are one.
   Ibid.

In der Logik ist nichts zufällig
Nothing in logic is coincidental.
   Ibid.

Was ist dein Ziel in der Philosophie? Der Fliege den
Ausweg aus dem Fliegengas zeigen.
What is your aim in philosophy? To show the fly the
way out of the fly-bottle.
   Philosophische Untersuchungen

Wovon man nicht sprechen kann, darüber muß man
schweigen.
We should keep quiet about that of which we cannot
speak.
   Tractatus logico-philosophicus

Walther von der Vogelweide (1170-1230)
Beitet unz iuwer jugent zergê:
Swaz ir in tuot, daz rechent iuwer jungen.
Wait until your youth is gone! Your children will
reckon with you for what you did to them.
   Die Veter habent ir Kint erzogen.

Daz si dâheizent minne, de ist niwan senede leit.
That which they call love is nothing but yearning
sorrow.
   Daz si dâheizent Minne

Diu werlt ist ûzen schoene, wîz grüene unde rôt,
Und innân swarzer varwe, vinster sam der tôt.
The world is beautiful on the outside: white, green
and red; but it inside it is black and dark as death.
    Elegy (or Palinode)

Ich bin ze lange arm gewesen âne mînen danc.
I have been poor for too long against my will.
    Ich hân mîn Lêhen

Jâ leider desn mac niht gesîn,
Daz guot und weltlich êre
Und gotes hulde mêre
Zesamene in ein herze komen.
Unfortunately it is not possible for wealth and worldly
honour and God's grace all to come together in one
heart.
    Ich saz ûf eime Steine

Mâc hilfet wol, friunt verre baz.
Kinsmen may help, but friends are better.
    Man hôchgmâc

Möhte ich verslâfen des winters zît!
If only I could sleep through the winter time!
    Uns hât der Winter geschât über al

Ouwê war sint verswunden alliu mîniu jâr?
Where have they disappeared, all my years?
    Elegy (or Palinode)

Swer guotes wîbes mine hât,
Der schamt sich aller missetât.
Whoever has the love of a good woman will be
ashamed of every misdeed.
   Einneuwer Sumer

Waz hât diu werlt ze gebenne
Liebers dan ein wîp,
Dez sende herze baz gefruwen müge?
What dearer thing has the world to offer than a
woman who can gladden a yearning heart?
   Waz hât diu Werlt?

Kurt Weill (1900-50)
Die Nachwelt ist mir gleichgültig – ich schreibe für heute.
I don't care about posterity – I am writing for today.

Christoph Martin Wieland (1733-1813)
Das alte romantische Land.
The old land of romance.

Friedrich Wilhelm IV (1795-1861)
Ich liebe eine gesinnungsvolle Opposition.
I love an opponent with convictions.

Kaiser Wilhelm I (1797-1888)
Ich habe jatzt keine Zeit, müde zu sein.
I've no time to be tired.

Kaiser Wilhelm II (1859-1941)
Der Tag.
The Day.
> *A pre-First World War toast, referring to the anticipated outbreak of war*

Herrlichen Tagen führe ich euch entgegen.
I am leading you towards wonderful times.
> *February 1892, to the provincial state parliament of Brandenburg*

Ich kenne keine Parteien mehr, ich kenne nur Deutsche.
I no longer recognise political parties; I recognise only Germans.
> *4 August 1914, to the Reichstag in Berlin*

Johann Joachim Winckelmann (1717-68)
Die edle Einfalt und stille Größe der griechischen Statuen ist zugleich das wahre Kennzeichen der griechischen Schriften aus den besten Zeiten.
The noble simplicity and calm greatness of the Greek statues are also hallmarks of Greek writing in the best periods.
> *Werke*

INDEX

A